Time to Get Here: Selected Poems 1969–2002

IAN PATTERSON was born in 1948 and grew up in Cheshire and London. He edited or co-edited *The Curiously Strong, Greedy Shark, A Vision Very Like Reality* and *Holophrase*. After a variety of jobs, he now teaches English at Queens' College, Cambridge. He has published numerous translations, most recently *Finding Time Again,* the final volume of Proust's *In Search of Lost Time* from Penguin. He lives in Cambridge with the writer Jenny Diski.

Time to Get Here

SELECTED POEMS 1969–2002

IAN PATTERSON

SALT

PUBLISHED BY SALT PUBLISHING
PO Box 937, Great Wilbraham PDO, Cambridge CB1 5JX United Kingdom
PO Box 202, Applecross, Western Australia 6153

© Ian Patterson, 2003

The right of Ian Patterson to be identified as the
author of this work has been asserted by him in accordance
with Section 77 of the Copyright, Designs and Patents Act 1988.

First published 2003

Printed and bound in the United Kingdom by Lightning Source

Typeset in Swift 9.5 / 13

ISBN 1 876857 92 7 paperback

SP

1 3 5 7 9 8 6 4 2

For Jenny

Contents

Acknowledgments

This book includes poems written over the last three decades, many of them not previously gathered in book form. For their support and for the first publication of these poems, I would like to record my thanks to the following:

Peter Ackroyd, Anthony Barnett, Fred Buck, Cambridge Conference of Contemporary Poetry, Cambridge Poetry Festival, David Chaloner, Andrew Crozier, Philip Crozier, Nate Dorward, Allen Fisher, Paul Green, John James, John Kinsella, Tim Longville, Tony Lopez, the late Barry MacSweeney, D. S. Marriott, Rod Mengham, Drew Milne, Julia Mishkin, Wendy Mulford, the late Philip O'Connor, the late Douglas Oliver, Tom Raworth, Peter Riley, Peter Robinson, Stephen Rodefer, Aidan Semmens, Iain Sinclair and Picador, Martin Thom, Nick Totton, John Tranter, Nigel Wheale, and others.

Thanks too to Brian Callingham for scanning the cover picture, and to Chris Emery for his exemplary helpfulness and enthusiasm.

Section One 1969–1979

Poem

to take up a position as
part of the space you perceive
                turn your back there is
infinite unconscious where I used
to be standing. into which you might
(if an unwary step back)
from the window, fall. with a rain
slipping sidewise in under your eyelids
sad russell street sloping right away
upwards
              a tenure in earth
beside indifferent trees numerous puddles
A rusty wheelbarrow the disordered remnants
of a childhood & one wellington boot
      the sky wd not be any sort
of plane surface nor a single depth
no, full of its own angular exteriority
'a triumph of advanced geometry' & partly
made of brick, and is how you would see us
                even if only
                momentarily

The Elegy for Spring

We have then no mark but
this damp smell which has
enlisted the daffodils the tulips
the wallflowers & the grass
the chestnut trees under
stonework. the guardians of peace
beautiful as a hundred horsemen
dance about the salad/ their red capes.
Have they heard of the Tragedy?
they show no signs of admitting
but "OH! see the arch of the roof
the anger of the butterflies
the knees of the young girls!
dive to them, they are small down there
& your hunger surpasses the sunlight
for merely the look of them . . . "
the sky is scarlet &
palpitates at our feet:
the systole is a deceptively gentle action
and as I burn I suddenly realise
being illusory & transitory it is
As interestingly as it began
the music stops. the meadows
float empty &
                Is that what the song of the eagles meant?
that these massive caves with
their brick arches are becoming
too hot: I shall get myself
another place to live, where
it will not be you?

Kara Chach

I

unwithered and gloriously thin-fingered, she is wrapped
    completely
encompassing horizon the park the street down to the river,
    hoping
what will happen tomorrow. She jumps into the air crinkling
slightly at the edges of choice ('until the day stone cut scissors')
who is after all not heroic, about to be beset with years of it, he
had to eat it. The door opens slowly
and putting down my fork to begin the journey.
Well, Dr. Wolfgang, has the hidden? we are still wondering
the flat river the liberty to watch them at war or otherwise, what
    have you to tell us?
How believable this scenery is/ 'The past, the sensations of the
    past!'
but this is only an excuse for something sandier, nearer to love.
How believable this scenery is/ 'The past, the sensations of the
    past!'
but this is only an excuse for something sandier, nearer to love.

II

Washing up noises from downstairs light again piles of books all
  round the
bed as usual I'm back again and it's Sunday. The problem of
  bookshelves
is still unresolved so I resolve to buy some wood tomorrow get
  things sorted
out I seem to have been using up an awful lot of distance lately
  like
travelling underground or anyway in a different kind of space
  though still
quite credible even attractive if you discount the fear the flat
  river
elms and sycamores glowing across permitted possibilities I
  traverse in
gumboots nightly. I mean Dragons, really, and the water rising
  maliciously
over the edge of the sink washing us out into this strange
  country with
nothing but lumpy earth and me dying of heartfailure gesturing
  delicately in
the hope of two doves; heroism? it's not even useful, I must get
  down to some-
thing useful, in fact the only known legacy that has come down
  to us there
is a common denominator in these ideas. Noises from
  downstairs again it's getting
darker already the screwdriver is too small the knots keep
  coming undone the
sauce won't thicken I seem to have been using up an awful lot of
  time lately
like travelling and dreaming about death and buses the past the
  sensations of
the past, Dr. Wolfgang has turned into an icon, I think I'll go and
  talk to Nick.

[6]

Quiet Arriving

It would certainly be best if we only counted to sixteen
this time. Remember they said blood was 'a splintery trap
as biological as they come'? well, with a careful titration
it can also help you puff achievement right out
into the freewheeling state
exactly as described on the back of the packet. So
switch off the engine—time to be up and doing, because
we're all off to the everglades.
                              Yes, she was listening. Her face
shines like an expectation fugue as a golden bird
swoops us up.
Everything is silent
and the swamps give way to the ocean
where a particular green becomes the order of the day.
Occasionally even the shadow of a gigantic seagull
is emblazoned across us, making dilutive forays into
penny-a-hundred disappointments. It's so easy to ignore!
                              Coming this way, we've avoided
battles and stolen a march on dozens of computer firms.
Lunchtime has mercifully become a thing of the past, all the
surrounding ringlets of lips absorbed, each into its own
        miniature
range of delights—and all this we are encouraged to call Friend
without the encumbrance of a legacy.
                              The wording shifts colour momently
here; blood on the grass blades slides liquidly off
while we touch ground where trust
is the whole fleet of our words, and even past it.

Summing It Up One of These Days

when you've been up all night for years
laying bare each vein
and yet the whole physiology
fades to dissolute marble,
does it hurt more than
Would you mind removing your hat?

> *Tableau*
> the ancient Carolina has been
> repainted in purpple, and
> here it comes, like an iron will o' the wisp,
> scrunching a bit
> like an earthquake in a bunch of violets
> then silence

Follow it. Plangently dance the bicycle
to the end of the world.

Ah! Flutes and buskins
all swallowed up now,
remember those times?
after supper on the verandah
and Saturday afternoons in the Boccherini Loggia
dreamily picking at his arms with a pair of scissors . . .

Oh, toot-toot, the vision is upon us.

> the same music clasps
> the fields to itself, singing
> "When you've a lizard in your pocket, love
> whispers politely of the perfect signature."

A Happy New Year

All a-corking in velvet coherence, it's
harder than it looks to leap from 1873 to the postbox but
we do try, and it's so elegant & smells, mmm . . . , familiar.
      All the seventy guns (or such) are out of action;
biding time; *he's* hung up his school cap for good,
determined to cut a figure in the world. Well,
    thin ice these January days.
I don't believe in it myself: flowers occurring near
the dawn-out boundaries of each marshy sentence. Still,
live there until the time comes, eh?
                         Perhaps it was condescending
of them to implicate me—they all sail so close under
the meniscus of hope
                the slightest touch would be Bungle.
Another thing, whose consideration is at the root of this?
Local days to manipulate, hours of syrtic conversation, we're
all like policemen footing it through yards of treacle.
   Oh, we sail on, affecting nonchalant unconcern
that each meal contains its own version of the last one:
yesterday's recipe was about fudge. Just a few fracid moments
between the years, then suddenly it's all fallen away.
               A kitchen landscape you entered
                another black telephone to pick up and
you considered my voice as it were an
embryo pearl to be picked up among the grass; in
itself your own heart discarding alternative tints
to come down fair and square in favour of dawn green.
What was that gesture again? Really?

Waking Up: 2.10 pm

The ground is white, four
walls of the courtyard are white,
the white sky is white
                    Only
              the balls on the white croquet lawn
                        over there
are blue,
              hier in Deutschland.

Politics

the sinking disc inside my eyeball
is solacing itself with gorgeous amber dregs
and the crumbs from a penguin biscuit
scatter like little rabbits I shoot with my teeth

daft Corsican. A patchwork figurine
bobbing in blue water
writing long letters home to be sent in bottles
and tickle the undersides of girls
who swim too far out
and will probably not deliver them.

pull out the thud of hatchets
if you want to be a man.

there are weeds at the bottom of my glass
and my spine is crashing

Marigold, Marigold
are you a freedom fighter?
do you come childless from Bangla Desh?
did you arrive by bus or
were you driven from your country
by an unconditional matter of tattered stucco?

Night Ministry

I glow like a berry
fire about my head
night putting a
porcelain white
seal on the grass

the mouth
nibbles a pudding
and the teeth
snarl enlarged in
the sponge

the nostril
splendid
as grapes
suspended over
me

woolly
fleecy as wool
field of the brain
fire about the head
smoke between
pricking
the eyes

Lullaby

She sleeps for health in terraced cities
banding out note after note evenly
pacifying the tin flies and the sundials
she is the only honest threader.

if I turned over a scarlet portion
difficult fingering makes it slow
because you smile to find your union
and no doubt to relinquish secrets.

blow the trickled music comfortably
and let me hurl accomplishment the wheel
until pins foregather like the hyades
the sweeping monitors of graft.

Ritual Slips

Increase the strong allowances at Easter
and watch it burn, the wood you only love
as flames that twist under neatness all the size

Having each acratic shade of blue
smeared on my temples made me a dreamer
and I buckled on my picnic

Never encountering the piano's rigour
where the sand finished the shrimps up
in what was portraiture of ivories

He started wrong: the haste it took
was planted early and the jug beside his foot
a bleak survey in and out of buckets

A curving hedge to grow from it
that stood as gristle to the next question
the nesting whitethroat's lamp

Believing lunch was ready on the handle
I meant you. Who feathers your lip?
that have planted this herb of incipient violet.

Polly Fortune

it's a late basket underneath
the bottled aspect of the rhododendrons

my sword taints each hand I lay
to the quillon this evening

over the bridge her treading
is to each speedwell like a mottled egg

through the factory wall
another square where the French drink

my shoes have grown up aslant
& bent the grass

Red Breath

you flop to me tonight
when the clutttered table floats
over the bass line in these small hours

you increase like volume
and water me from your padded skull

you turn coracles of scaly wonder
as your legs steady up
into my fat larder

what pain there was
you fly it like a flagman
busy with the red fern

and you reach for the starver
in king needles of even breath.

Hold the Child, Father Sunlight

The new months are blown until
the Kent coast sharpens where we file
it into our returning eye

spiced up into a colder light
to marching yellow faces
a sea full of terns for a socket

I persuaded some to liberty among
nettles for tickets to your proud teeth:
Hold the child, father sunlight, to the greater canvas

while the instant of colour stays
where we were, mud-crowned to the nines,
and knew the way and the blue expanse.

A Thing of Reason

PENCIL

At the back of the building sacks empty,
lemon fills my eyes with tears; such is
the music of restoration in your hands
spread like teeth before a blind composer.
Faultless drizzle from the fountain cuts
arches about you: anxiety hangs in it
ripe for my bunches of fingers; alert
it pulls the white stick, the fox is afraid,
low cloud obscures your last envelope. Carry
what you can. Outline your eyes with poppyseed
as you leave me. I'll wait in the kitchen.
Sweet houseflies will predict the dissolution
of an order from this heap of patois: only
outside a pencil stalks the implacable day.

FATAL CONGERIES

A lost view ungums my lips, matches
this coat of painted wood, horns are sprout-
ing, this head of mine sings uncontrollably
of woodland sawbenches & the figure of my
grandfather. Eagle feathers lie about under
the table picturing a weak climax to a
long chain of feathered betrayal; as I sleep
I lose all my visions into a pot of
goose and celery stew. Go on, march as you
smoulder, it's the smell of your boots I
love through all the century's smells. If
a thousand neckscarves are waved on a day like
this, the earth shudders and arms itself
for entire bodies to walk into the consequence.

As We Run Out of the Wet

you," she said. I'm cast as matter, an over-
mirror of your waving barley
long meeting between the teeth
what did my fingers, a man
Also I eat wild things, what did
Book showing a single logic. I
it sat quietly and ate my brain

MAN

A tremendous glitter widens my opinion of
the war beyond her thin grey face and my yellow
fingers. I am cheese; this plateau offers me
as a yellow cube. I refuse the darkness
and the sinuous attempts of promise in my
imagination half-governed and waving beside the
river like a nest of curly black hair that turns
to rain and pits me. I fall apart and
trickle down my forehead like a star.
I hear the grass at my knees coming.
Whatever has been eating the fern lies on canvas
and dreams of the stepping sheep; I put out
my hand from the trestle table and touching
its wool I am content to watch the town blown up.

Bound to a Time

Hope burns his hand on this concourse
listening for the law we round up and
eat off, those eyes a pitiful month
on my wall, a collar loose and white.
Wanting to go you raise your fist de-
riving the new grammar in a grand we; and
walk out pushing our bonhomie where the wet
men listen after years of hunger. All
afternoon I thought this was a delegation
of short words for struggle. Lunarcharsky
rises like the sun out of his overcoat;
the law, the cusps furnished reconstitution,
settle to the class of all things, his
hand raised where the bird flies, his face.

Japan is Sad

I put my eyes in trust whose inflected words
twitch on the table between us. They flicker, I am
not going to blow up the sheep, emblem of my
mortal love. Wear my clothes and it'll rain.
The unfortunate traveller whose feet we point
at the road is dead. Weep for him. Conform his
shape to your hands' air and ventilate his
sad hope as the fire is fanned with lexical beauty.
     It is the only sponge I have, this platform
and my breath makes it sway as it washes my features from
the code. What kind of mirror is it absorbs
light when my flames can be seen for miles? When
the sun rose advertising the moon in the words
of history, who turned from the east and smiled?

SENTINEL

Would a house by the lake, a small grammar of
silent looks win the struggle he wondered. A mythology
of faces can satisfy a need for clarity without
the burden of association we have known. Ears and tongues
mark out time as the women come and go, whose only
dream is the end of the world they invent as the laws
we leave behind whenever we spread our fingers to an
innocent flame burning in your eyes. Write the invention
of truth in your capable suggestions. They wave
like a vision
     and leave me fixed and not decaying
not a snapshot. Radical clauses exact no tribute
from the street; a day like this enfolds the inside
real moment in a clasp of inextinguishable sentiment.

REQUIEM FOR A BRAIN

Plunge your heart. The scarved
figures step out of hearing
to demand my reprieve. I will be
scanned and made to balance where
soaring hope fell between my teeth
and my breathless jaw. Oh let me
sing in nervous light, give me the
clay of skulls to work in free
afternoons. Will is nothing but
a thing of reason.

NOTES

Will is nothing but a thing of reason.

There are different ways of perceiving the world.

Nations are bound by the limits of a language.

Nobody but a nice girl loves a sailor.

Sparkling Fruit Salts

KINO

Never be alone. Cell
protein constructs its
narrative in the dark
& we sit taking in aerial
snaps of receptor sites
proper conditions of
sense whirring across
the surface of the reel
crime & every mounting
sentence resounds
appealing and falls flat
against the screen where
there is no conversation
blinding growth first
egg of history
flickers and proposes
a resolution of some
more celestial device

LINO

for Denis Roche

No admittance board gleamed above hedges
or nests of pippit rejoined the lost
cuckoo of summer, opening eyes in early sun-
light as re-entry into the forbidden
matter of dreams
such a future is inconceivable
amulet of tender stance useless against
my power of hatred and its speckled
vision collimated or transcribed for two
flutes and a barrel-organ. Buff
architecture like in Florence lacks the
lyric presence of granite. I wonder if
song is a mineral function of our material
chemistry crystallising the substance of
each ideational trace of our passing?

NINO

co-workers refuse offers of dis
junction appropriate to a landscape
of pineal variety more than the board
room where I thought your shape improper
your smartly groomed pubic hair verged
on the blasé veered off
that moment's utterance into buttercup
fields of your arse as memory
my linguistic referents laze in
polymorphous undergrowth scatt
ered in a corner of my research
casamatta where I escape floods and
bombs and the thud thud of pine
cones fruitless occasions the surf
torn jacket shifting beneath the surf
ace of a role she might see as im
personal amid miscellaneous visions
mirrors confronting an innocent
subject with its constant
business of living

Rhino

eye this tragedy of
unmasked circumstance pink
faces reveal trembling leaves
something to seize
hold on to removed
from actual life
would you allow me
an encyclopaedia a neigh
bouring bed in the
munitions plant
ation? Quick hide geranium
seed floating formally
acquitted but still
guilty oral or not to
carry your house on your
foolish back grind
your horn the pool of
reminiscence I regard
as my amorous history
we inhabit as
ground it all thunders
with its approach

VINO

Effractive light falls
on her from its
source behind the lens
breaks and simply pours
glass after glass
enough to limit
pressure on the round
fruit rinsed of cog
nition in such baths
of what seems like
pure planes of what
I always thought
I ever knew
would contain it all.

The Yurt: Day One

1. THAT THE PERSONAL QUALITIES HE HAD GAINED IN THIS WAY BELONGED

From the cities. From other places. Twelve arrived for the three days.

"An *aitys* demanded great resourcefulness and, most of all, an ability to improvise." The choice includes abuse, panegyric, mockery and exchanges (contests) of wisdom and knowledge. I excluded, as degenerate, competitive collective form work.

The yurt was rapidly assembled, metal and skin among others, mind interface. A tent of thought for mutual habitation and pleasure. "that those poets whose / mental level does permit them to / know order". The weather is always important.

2. BY VIRTUE OF ITS LIMITATIONS, IN OTHER WORDS BY VIRTUE OF A

"But far more mightily than by the past is the mind influenced by the future; the former leaves behind only the quiet perceptions of remembrance, while the latter stands before us with all the terrors of hell . . . " (Feuerbach). All those who wanted to live in another world, the situational architecture of the yurt, the moment of grazing, came hesitant and more or less cynical to the place, on the grounds that they were going in that direction anyway. So much for intense local seriousness, local is caused by social time. Our mouths opened in uncertain speech, advent of hope ("many of the events referred to under the catch-all term 'tone of voice'") walked, skinned up, had a drink.

3. THE WAR WAS IN THE LAST EVENT AN ANTICLIMAX

Everybody retired to Berne library to read *The Science of Logic*. Art. Nick said he didn't think much of *High Pink on Chrome*. (None of the Old Ones were at the yurt, although Mike Haslam found some footprints near the stream. We were deeply concerned over their presence in the yurt's fabric in case there was a storm.) I argued staying at home, risking the very simplest food, entering the field through elevated rehearsals of the music of paraconceptual possibilities unavailable to the ordinary neurologist. In five-dimensional space, the music of the spheres demands an improvisatory topology, the internal surface of the world, the roof of the yurt.

4. OBLIGATIONS OF HIS OWN CONFIRMED HIS FEELING

"that the Mind or Will always

successfully opposes & invades the Previous"

It was an argument that began. The set text was *Lud Heat*, nobody knew whether Iain Sinclair would arrive, whether he had already been translated or if he was there like the missing things hidden somewhere in the picture. Si tu penses pour les autres, ils penseront pour toi. For this session the yurt was urban, and nothing changed. Martin accepted the 'danger of metal finish', I wanted to talk about Tatlin's dream.

The frame of our temporary world expanded, its central geometry became clear to all. But it was only a sign.

5. ON ONE'S CHEEKS

Schwitters's magazine *Pin* never got off the ground. It was intended to be the hole people had to creep through to see what art is all about. We all agreed to oppose creeping. I am introducing this to you. It is not my place to offer homage. I wear a beard, which I keep short. Next to arrive were Nigel Wheale and John Seed:

"the human eye, when, inside it does not know
any more than what it can express by living &
that sight be in this man's eye is the expression we call love:"

6. HALF OF ALL HUMAN ASSERTIONS SIMPLY CANNOT BE TAKEN SERIOUSLY

What's more, I must explain that these chapter headings are taken, by means of a random number sequence provided by Deborah, from Volume 1 of *The Man Without Qualities*, which was also chosen randomly, and were not discussed at any stage during the yurt itself.

7. FIGHT

a possible explanation of our joint presence was proposed by this heading. We reject it for its connotations of violence without hurt. We formed a circle facing outwards and chanted "a dream is constructed by the whole mass of dream thoughts being submitted to a sort of manipulative process in which those elements which have the most numerous and strongest supports acquire the right of entry into the dream content", while inhibitory theories of cortical activity circled around.

8. DOWN WAS NOTHING COMPARED TO THE REALITY

Ian reported on his visit to the Ian Tyson exhibition at the Tate, where in order to see the prints he had had to clamber round people eating lunch. Four people had moved their meals to other tables or other parts of the same table, one had complained loudly, and another had had his coffee spilt by the viewer as he stepped back suddenly from 'field of blood, sound of wave'.

9. AMONG THE FEW MEN WHO HAD AN INFLU-

Peter Philpott introduced the session on the search for pleasure. He began by quoting Einstein: "Behind these essays lies above all an epistemological requirement which derives from the gestalt-psychological point of view: beware of trying to understand the whole by arbitrary isolation of the separate components or by forced or hazy abstractions." Martin came in with some words of Engels from *On the Housing Question*: "really being in love means wanting to live in another world [. . .] The orgasm [. . .] is a glimpse of a transformed universe." By now it was late afternoon, misty and dusky, and the walks were over.

10. THE FOLLOWING PAGES FROM A LETTER

" . . . the decadence of former notions of public presence, idealistic communities, etc., is exposed." Perhaps you would agree, though, that *that* proposition is really based on the idea that they aren't, that functioning, localized energy is more than just the historical path it assumes, takes into itself the rejected idea, is self-defining as continuity rather than revolution? Attached to this note is the resolution agreed by seven of the twelve who came to the yurt, on the future of painting. What do you think about point iii?

11. SAME ENDLESS FORCE, SWEPT TO LEFT AND RIGHT

I think your readers will probably find that heading self-explanatory. By late evening the yurt was complete, the constructional geometries of Spinoza and Einstein had succeeded in providing complete twelvefold siamese thought shelter. (cf esp. *Ethics*, Part III Prop LV, Note 1.) We sat in silence and prepared Day Two and Day Three.

12. HAD HAPPENED FOR THE FIRST TIME HOW HIGH THE SKY REALLY WAS

Tatlin's Dream

CURIOUSLY STRONG

for Fred Buck

Contact at shops at bus stops at places where we
drink stars shining bright in the little sky and hum
of the dominant series in both ears no bees could lift
my head off like this music will not stop and getting louder
my field of vision shrinks and optic nerve strains
cannot deliver the goods they get too big for their boots
and while not laughing or growing any other way men and
    women
I don't know enlarge their hair-crowned heads to bend towards
me words and memory-assaults. It will take the curious
strength of a moment of thought to recoil from the impending
    tone
and hate with effort and critical severity sentences
employed like us as advertisements as warnings now to
    appropriate
the sentences employed for ephemeral consumption of the
    central
personality, the tune of the market piped into a booming sound
of slippers on the pavements as the sky glooms over and dour
afternoon clouds gather above the isle of dogs,approach of
more domination huge face of no response no traveller returns
unless the sales we are proceed and grow our enormous soul
    chopped
into splinters who populate and are the concrete
potentials unhandled by the touch of vision behind her national
health spectacles oh minerva with the pointed frames on which
    no
star will rest until the day comes with the promise of no more of
    it

light and colour when they slip off the only
source there is, too late for actual use
past the moment of realisation, as tears
ran down his smooth face, enough finance
to protect him as he sleeps in sorrow
and the weather operates gently with snow
and other quiet things. And time in barrels
horseshoe marks in the turf, mud
and broken collarbones of November in the
money. No prison, only pain when I move it
and I may receive visitors. He was there
too long, the leather decayed. No tiring insistence
that the significance you create is the result
of a mediating process, wispy symbols of nationalist
intrigue, just a sky singing in an empty sky
as we watched the race from the heather
no—cancel & insert 'Colour is dealt with in
the language of colour in these large paintings:
do not talk to me again.' I looked down on the
course; above me the sky was clear, the light hard;
my boots glistened with wet; some of the almost
white sand coated the toe of each boot. It was
chalky. I will not say what I could hear
noises obtrude and represent pain of course. You
won't get a word out of me until I have stayed too long.
This is a silent blackbird photographed leaving
the stock exchange, this is the end of an era.

ANY OLD IRON

Pioneer comes back to the financial circuit,
transfuses its outlines. His value is false,
we all turn from his lines of primitive reception
as they grip the carpet and seep out into the street.
The sailor's dream is quashed under the rig,
       concrete slabs bob on the tide,
         the linear output function records another disturbance
                             among the welders.
Listen to easy predictions and measure
your historic displacement, Feathers float against the
dock, we can never give up. Across the dust of the barrier
is an object. Distance is a sentimental notion
but iron can't flop from language into language at
the whim of communal desire. The frame is less than we do.
We hold the arch over the scuffed path and vanish, no
self-organised state in the rolled-up sleeve except as it extols
the reach of a thing or a day. This is what we all desire
and fail to inscribe in our traces.

Note also the amusing attempts of the author and add
that this unity "money" is not something actual. Truth is
all-sided, of nature by man from moment to moment. What
is your favourite moment of cognition? Not yet developed,
not yet unfolded, perhaps a hint of vacillation here?
Under the heading "Ices of every description" they kept
shop, into space and time at the hands of expert layout
technicians. Could be earning a hundred or so minimum
somewhere else. But you'll remember "self-mediating movement
and activity" eh? Remember the glossy cigarette packet
too. Pull out the cigarettes *by means of* the gold tab
and offer them to all the persons present. *Proffer* your
lighter—it will save embarrassment. The universal is the
foundation, and burns clearly after dark.
Ignition? "The history of thought equals the history of
language??" (Lenin). Ah! The necessity of connection. The
international monetary fund and the traffic warden. A two
act play by Fernando Arrabal. Nobody can afford to see it.
I say nobody (embarrassed cough), I assume your basic
acceptance of the "immanent emergence of distinctions"
and the heavy germanic cast of your eyebrows. Do I
exclude the most germane, the gold glint on your wild wings?

Some Comfort

What do you want
from my mouth? Words?

There are no words.
Thought (if you'll excuse me)
is made everywhere
except the mouth

that pink excuse
rimmed with teeth.

Do you want my mouth? It's yours.
Engrave my teeth with slogans.

I have a memory of pale blue stripy mothers.

When the bald memory of the bald man shot himself
betrayed, I woke up.

Wake up! Wake up! Wake up!
All is not as it seems either in bed or out of it.

Do you have a bed?

"THE AUDIENCE"

The audience for a poem is silence. Listening
awakes somewhere inside you, and the language
spreads out till it has claimed your entire skeleton
and filled with its presence the volume your skin encloses

You don't absorb it. Like when some biologist injects
a blue dye into some small translucent organism
it's not absorbed. You become a perfectly controlled
airship, and sail into action like a musical phrase

'LIFE DREAMED IS NOW LIFE LIVED' (DAVID GASCOYNE)

black on white
the first up on the wall turned back
their glowing eyes
our thousands of feet
on the ground

what woke me this morning
in the middle of the bed
puffy clouds sailed past the window

the pylons on the hill
stretched like a stocking before
it's pulled over a face

a black stocking
on a white face

such clean straight lines
they might have come from you
and your blob of orange

DERRY

these gardens sharp and previously unextended
sense of the possible prints on the wet grass
wasted evenings completed by some arabesque
of guns and cameras and turning film waiting to
go home piled injustice burning outside the flats
and the shapes it all takes look rather like us

The Political Economy of Art

You will see the good housewife
taking pride in her
pretty tablecloth,
and her glittering shelves,
no less than
in her well-dressed dish,
and in her full storeroom;
the care
in her countenance
will alternate with gaiety,
and though you will reverence her
in her seriousness,
you will know her
best by her smile.

Underground

for Peter Ackroyd

here's your address
    it glows apprehensively
       & undertakes a relaxation of personal work
         up in the sun
where the act of striking breaks hearts . . .
    the bicycle is binding too
    loves to hear you sing
       as maps unfold the summer
we call out hopefully as if the tune was dead
       only axles clutter the yard
      like fieldfares later on.

I tell you how I feel
       over something to drink in Southwark
    and watch your expression contract;
       the first results came up on the screen
          those drunken wires
grassing it out in other coppices
and beside reservoirs in the pennines:
       here's your economy, bone by bone,
     & I shall not stop undermining
          these children of europe or book you as
the season's distraction
    look there's the drop now
    I know you'll confront it.

Looking at Henry

Our unavoidable fate   not the Surrealists, the door
  deeming energy our purity masquerade.
                  Pearls hover, the last post
      is flattery
        and the path of the militia in winter
    lost under the snowfall
from a neck:
             no question of force
        of will, or writer's cramp.
The bends of space and time *is* not,
  it *happens*
          without distance in light;
so much for defiance—
Nothing will ever stop people meeting each other's eyes

  That's safe, an assertion from above, and
none the less true for that.
Conquest. A condition
      of perfectly neutral word
      that already exists in the block.
It makes no difference to Henry, owning the dream,
    dreaming it from wall to wall,
        if he eats the eye
          like a stocking before it's pulled over a face.
Just a peak of actual surfaces, your crystal-clear intentions
        and his moral imagination
          together between the covers
a single impulse of inept combination.

Endless Demands

After how
this wound
close when
I was thought
on my knee
is history. The
history of
my memory
is not
in the corner
of my
change in this.

The Chronicler

A replica city
glass meets eye and sees through it
hands rub over the pavement

curling into names
that control the city
basking in dry grass

cylindrical plane trees
in the jointed evening
men rule lines

surrounded by paper and metal
you might decide to discard the air
How unearthly!

or fall under that gaze
plate glass, leather, pink fingers
force to force as they scream

replica time
in the Greenwich web
oscillating at some unlikely frequency

Talking 'Bout Things

Congealed air at the windows in June making
all our time burst like sweat behind my shoulders

a million grass seeds water the garden
in a hose of dust, a display of bleeding

breathless and gritty politics of the photographic present
books flower and fade and I forget them. It was 96 degrees.

It was not true although we call it sleep. Attractive bulb
rash Shelleyan flutter, tie the windows with string

le monde rentre dans un sac. You said you had to go to sleep
and did it, falling to type up your life on a sample pillow

Garden herb more nameless than a vision of it
by what it leaves out, hung and dried for the jar

We sidle about, keeping our minds on money, broadcast
utter failure of purchased hope. They lost it all.

Brief on the hoof it was, legs crossed by the stairs against peeling
blue. Our hot child breathes. The myths in the air make me
        tired.

THINGS REPLY

If I close one eye
I remember migration
into fiery trees

feet straight him
little sparrows and a starling
no pigeons

lazy ideas
tremble on your breath
like beads of water

slivers of yellow
language which
teaches itself

I am overcome
and go home to
white, grey, black

Apprehension

The grasping skeleton
divides rooms, wallpaper paste,
repeats until my eye is blunt
Are you there? Force. Axons pioneer
routes of time and sympathy,
capillary indecision
blurs the industrial delta.

What is the object of living here?

Arriving for the day shift
as it dawns the modern age
reappears in the words of this street
the object is an object for everybody
as it dawns, the single, public light.

HARDLY YIPPEE

over miles of flat land
blows the concrete dust

red and white things
in the forsaken windows

his long legs volunteering
his heart for the future

they never installed "correct breathing"
a lack which pleased the critics

huge clouds pass
like dungarees

in his hands was his head
in his head was his heart

along the minute rifling
were inscribed the words

"we now know that work should be
man's most beautiful occupation"

there is no such thing
as preparation for construction

WE MUST TIGHTEN OUR BELTS

cold blue mouth clenched
as determinate origin
no kidding

just having a long conversation
silence descends quicker
than we think

and placid the scissors lie
on the paper
I forgot to ask

difficulties on the inter-city
out of the backwoods
dense tufts of pine

distance hits the window
I am heaved
into the future

like the smug curve of mortgage interest
into the balance of the proud father
of a nation warming to his job

nothing in my head
      unknotting my fingers by the border
  I am the return of the rhyme
               you can
         call me Miriam this time
      with a vengeance
            at the door with a bunch of lovage
         at the window to unknot my view
on the march
       to midsummer
            and the finished product
              in the brass.
      A key turns
    in the marmite jar
          like telepathy from
     a passing car

LIGHT DETERMINES A STATE OF ABSOLUTE REST

You need to have a transformation
        formula to relate this to that and language
            shaken apart as a matter
of exchange
      rising at seven to the cupboard
      blade cooked up to prevent it.
This vice of thought
  was sweating for a tin-opener
    as I remember it
like a mould fringe on a picture in the townhall
or a size cut too small from the inside.
      They have trampled to the moon
          for a young delivery of news
              on the open market
         and come back with
     lino cuts.
Fundamental uneasiness about this a state of mind, then,
      in time for it.

OUT OF DATE

Today an overt hunger for unity
sweeps between them and
returns to apply white thoughts
to the business of our next impulse
but lets it drop
               into a great vacuity
the crowd's idea of Australia
                or the disc of a sun bottle
everyone watches it fly over
like a second home
        balancing a bucket
            in the reflection of a ticket
        at which point they realised that the solution
              of the "problem" involved
            a redefinition of the customary concept of time.

It Was a Long Lane

Bricks beckon irreducibly
to heat up, colourless scream,
or condense our programme
for photographing pain
in a bridge to cognition interference—
a minute of psyonic cantilever
among thousands against hundreds
a more open gesture
dropping charges with sentiment
utter mess, pure food, organic prelude,
max overdraft on rehearsed information
and the rest of the lunchtime
entertainment team will stay away.

I Felt a Hand Grip My Elbow

All right, the air is full of lies
and you breathe it, desire them
from the first
getting a measure of our sobbing
inelegance from the yellowed writings
of the permawar philosophers.
Our familiar phlegm lurks on the membrane
too smart to take up the struggle
from the soiled discs,
luminous faces in the tube
a swagger of cultural politics
in the cradle of tubular men
with no response to the rest
but quietly determined to unleash the silly hatchet
on its one-way journey to the burial ground
and harness the relentless pulp
to a word in someone's ear
to find out about you, I mean
you don't like it either, do you?

IN YOUR FACE

Then there was vegetable satire, a
lonely subject snarled on star-time
without money for a facelift
or a tool of thought
with studs on the inside
limit—it's all they had
until war entered the canopy of their wildest dreams
singing some Cole Porter number in
a storm like third-hand Shakespeare in a shopping bag.

Turn to the left, turn to the right,
turn to the stars as they
shine all night
like a bone in your teeth it's
home for the beast in your bath.

And that distilled resentment
that satirical old erection
keeps the whole show on the road
year after year.

Endless Demands

Oh don't you start, it's
    a discrete mode of address
        full of numbers
      steel noise at the edge
  of a vertical band
        and the stolen letter
      strict and remote
    fluttering from the pointed lie.
            The sky stops
        with a lyrical fist-stagger
              and your mouth is
    already manufacturing a world.
   Everyday demands
      is a good deal to take
without an entirely extra coming war
        without history
              or music
         or work on one alternative
          after conceiving
          the thought experiment.
     But the chips are
            down, the
               word is out.

In 1938

This morning I went back
to the bay window
a feverishly retreating future
in a street of fallen angels
of bells and sounds
in the bleak trees
& dirty privet
thin light with
ink over
on the corner
where mouths exchange
greetings & greed
as a darkness approached
and I looked out
at unrelieved war
nothing to do about it
and lived through
glassy and
boundless the deep
and narrow passage of
what I have done

Section Two *Roughly Speaking*
Poems from the 1980s

One morning I walked back through the park, and saw the highest branches of a tree draped with bits of marabout, with some sort of silk, with two or three odd stockings and, wrapped round the top of the treee, like a cloak quick-thrown over the shoulder of some high-born hidalgo, some purple damask. Below it, balanced on a twig as if twirled round a finger, was a brand new bowler hat. They had all been blown across the road from the bombed hotel opposite. A surrealist painter whom I knew slightly was staring at this, too. He said: "Of course we were painting this sort of thing years ago, but it has taken some time to get here."

INEZ HOLDEN, IT WAS DIFFERENT AT THE TIME

Dans un monde unifié on ne peut s'exiler. Qu'ai-je donc fait pendant ce temps?

GUY DEBORD, PANÉGYRIQUE

All Our Ends

There is something to be said
As the forms cough in the cold street

We need to know what it is
And we wait for a voice in the words

As we look at imperialism in the glass
Hearing the wrong white words

The early crocusses listen in sudden frost
That wraps us in anticipation

The face on the screen looks back at me
And says "this is the being that started the necessary conflict

The world is also in him, and the words
Make space for it, if he struggles to listen

Absorbing and opening to it in the tide
Of everything he is. Are you ready?"

Discountenanced, the dead voice stops.
Corn dust and clutter fall lightly everywhere

Coating distrust and social engineering in a single thought
Of all our ends, so that it also fills our mouths.

Still Life

Reconsidering the track that parts the wind
as black thirst when there's nowhere else
but the necessary pain of women
ever to be found among other lines

when chanting like a leaf keeps you awake
and images are defined by torn sound
and a few stops in the pitch dark
afternoon light the merest streaming memory

some earthly fear afoot on stones and eyes
and what if your hands are full of a stifled voice
like guilt night after night saying don't give up
crowds are rising inside me on the line

these were the days lost in guesswork
and careful production of the stars
the women I mentioned chiselled the material
and laminated all the time in the world

at that period the water was all painted grey
the swan and its white shadow was outside
as white as arctic silence with both eyes open
and snow teeth instead of lashes

Without Rhyme or Reason

I may be without rhyme or reason
I may be watched by eyes of consequence
I may be the idea of the future shimmering like a summer
      holiday
I may be shrouded in a defiant haze
I may be driving from place to place
I may be pictures browning at the edges
I may be unjustifiably bad-tempered
I may be controlled by hidden strings or more likely not
I may be reflected expectantly in their unsubdued eyes
I may be turning over a new leaf
I may be on the night train or on the television news
I may be a conceptual possibility
I may be like they always did before
I may be walled in
I may be like multiple speech
I may happen very naturally
I may be looks that have lingered
but roughly speaking I cannot be unchanged

It Had to Be You

When you watch a Spanish movie, you can speak it,
but you have to abandon everything.
What you imagine you empty of thought and lines of beauty
& what you do is joined to the dead hours.
          Grey light falling on naked angles.
I shall break on you, too. Day thumps with a heavy step.
What you (you) imagine is neither here nor there
and we are both in between it together.
          Now where? The view (of clean lake and damp earth)
might be a specifically male one,
with entwined postcards on a sable ground.
It will become too dark for words:
belly of sleep with its humble fingers in the butcher's tray.

What you do right is dissatisfaction but the reasons are wrong.

Can you imagine that? A recognition shock stumbles over system
          and details
the confusion of waking up by the smashed frame.
Long walks beneath enamel moons. A scrabbling at the interior.
The edgy constancy of nerves and wet stares.
I can see it from the root to the stem. My vision is terrible.
Could you wake for anything more? You know where it all comes
          from.
You? I could have seen the memory coming.
Magic words never make any sense. Infinitudes alive to the dead
          hours.
Tortures in their proper places. Speech.

It happens, when I open the drawer of your clean and nameless
          voice.
What you imagine is fringed in dentistry and nailed to music
and splattered into the social. Me too. Or then teeth in my fist.

Everyone (you) spoke the language just as good. Can you imagine
          that?

The Origins of Love and Hate

Cross-grained dark
falls to a lost gasp

high-stepping irony floods
from television screens

particles of being invaded
regroup in a soft aura

against the light of years
choked by perennial systems.

Open another window, and another,
as yet such brilliant flower-heads ghost

in misted focus played
out on the boards

all the faces turn to each and laugh
huskily in the playbacks

witness to the artless cranesbill
of mellow self-deception

and sleeping half-life,
exposure too good for me

though what the barren hillsides
were for otherwise I can't imagine.

Late Capital

Not much light
left nostalgia
instead of hair
both sides of the cloud
multiple lost
end collapsed
run round and round
in furry darkness
buttered up for
special treatment
oil in the ear
in a compact
a freewheelin approach
he said, he said it
in a voice like wet fur

Irreducible Blue

Still day extends the line
and cajoles the bows in harmony
across the bone, across the street
till a sign of life stops the bike
or am I only romanticising
a simple journey to an end
suddenly in view and never out of it
now and in the singing night
and the singing dawn
your grace so present
these terrible times as
to have an attack of heart
and jump down from the blazing roof
all rescued from the frantic calm
of not writing by surprise and inspiration
so I'll do it, whatever it is,
because of you. This isn't it
but it is what I've tried
to make it by
typing against the bone
chorus sweetly deaf in life
as leaves return
(they bide their time at night)
in a fire of worry before the early
milkman calls across the street
with reassurance for the guttering
flame that seeks a way to ease and a hand up.

So to Speak

Heroes easily run a ground on reasons
but they're insatiable among the relics
of flame and light
or else they look up and see what's in the air

Nature spars with the profit motive
until cool waters are dulled
and everyone's eyes look as dead as last year
with its echo mirroring the skies

Humans like us are taken up with things
and every step we take
needs a little bit of blindness
or a man on the road to a port

As dispirited as surrealism
we may drop into a sort of reverie
where bells ring for no good reason
and voices emerge from faces

Some heroes love to hear
their chains rattling
inside them
on the way to meetings

Often they speak the language
but use thought as a whip
against the hands of time
so to speak

They also crumple things up
crush them inside and out
and then appear surprised
when they can't find the edge.

Speaking of Life

Frail dust in the bloodflow
not answering the door behind my eyes

some fracas stifles a cry at every corner
plaster images crumble and vanish

I wanted to shake off your presence
and I got lost on the way here

I thought someone was following me
but it was all there was to me when I arrived

to deface a picture of a man
without taking his feet off the ground.

After Breakfast

Somewhere else in the time spectrum
sweet morning drips from the line
white yogurt to ease my throat
I caught it on a nail I almost said
thorn although it was your eyes
that caught my breath and made me pause

Appeased by food I was attacked
by resentment and became something else wrong
with the world I was not born to get
it right I muttered through tense teeth
knowing that we should fight for what we love
not are, twenty years since Frank O'Hara died

In this world of intersecting manifolds
of power and circulation it is simply good
that after-images that change or remain
in the night or day should keep flowing
and never be the same twice
the flowers metamorphosis to the flood

i.e. the poem, which is the opposite
of an ark but sings at your gait
against the iridescent pages of modernism
descending a staircase or starting a car
forwards in the garage of the twentieth century
which looks unlikely but is the only way out

This is not literally true but I
have chosen all the statements freely
and do not a prison make even when hallucinations
hover round my heart and ears at night
or by day become coincidences of such beauty
I could weep at not believing in horoscopes

Prattle

Close darkness warms
my skin towards the thought
of you that keeps
flowing as my heart
keeps going as bodies
seem to I can lie
to myself to sleep

You Never Said

Don't say the light's going
shadows growing as the wind gets up
and owls at the gate

Don't say the dead hours are out again
beating at the shutters
like a heart with serious doubts

Don't say anything that sounds like a word
breaking over the track under winter branches
beside a deaf person with milky eyes

Don't say what's up
wasting night after night
monitoring the death of sunlight

Don't say too much about the past
things you loved bleeding all round the house
moments when years suddenly freeze.

Time How Short

> There is a Moment in each Day that Satan cannot find,
> Nor can his Watch Fiends find it; but the Industrious find
> This Moment & it multiply, & when it once is found
> It renovates every Moment of the Day if rightly placed.
> WILLIAM BLAKE

RED PRIEST

As in cotton frocks and bicycles
barley trembles in the moody, wonderful air

What we walk in not a photograph
clenched in other desperate hands
slowly the air thickens

Rain not anywhere still
in this passionate suspense

INTERFERENCE

Listen, what I won't say
or could deny the words mean
lines of scruple or waste
the merest roof
to hear winds
burning river of ignorance
reluctant to mean
to the crime of sound
or mind to reach reason
then swept out of the frame
heels flaming on the stones
of the site of this
this poor rendering
to say the least

MATTER AND MEMORY

Cloudy morning slides across today's indecision
everything's on my side except my veil
of nerves my vanity and speaking clock
encased in earlier images and untrue versions

I speak you wait something indecipherable
slowly changing masses shade into grey
softened by yellowish suggestions of budding leaves,
bring out a momentary shadow on the slates

coldly erased; bitter weeping within sight
down corridors of abandoned nature;
violets are mine, nature is blue, roses are like
a red, red pool

Likeness is not like a landscape, a
tract of fertility or menace laid
over brows of hills in wide brown clarity
and shadow: the moment repeats and repeats.

A Propos

A sundial in dawn mist
defining the virtues
what is a garden?

Shadow thought
a beech tree
nostalgic common sense

Spinning dreams in
later backdrop
the legislative wheel

These images are
thrown up in silhouette
on wild eyes

All this sadness
has orbital courses
not by way of despair

I must need
tremor of language
this isn't opaque

Anything musical
a minimum
eager for an absolute

In the split second
no more material
continues to unfold

I embrace you
this isn't opaque
it's autumn

II

Rain blows against the glass
there is an absent figure
in this composition

Leaves and water represent
slammed doors, hisses of breath
drenched in social relations

Rapid and insistent jabs of thought
like pigeons' necks on the platform
I would like the time please

Then the great relief of motion
with a purple-brown sweep of michaelmas daisies
in an abrupt light

Don't take your eyes off me
burning like the Alexandra Palace
on a horizon

Unproductive solitude
can be figured as rapid white paint marks
as flat as a wooden surface

You know this as it is spoken
it reveals a true moralism
I fall in with it straight away

Sleep or no sleep
the bristled skyline is stained
with hope to see my pilot face to face

How come primroses are out
beneath heavy branches of sloes
like a transparency of history?

TIME HOW SHORT

Voices like mosquitoes slant
past glasses
towards a dormer window
the fading pink light
claiming loudly it was the best
I could possibly have
so ist das Jahres Ende
I suppose similar people
drinking in a more self-consciously Scottish attitude
otherwise glazed in national inertia
shut up in a little room like this
all those years and the syringa or the buddleia
out of sight round the corner
occasionally a painted lady at the glass
or a peacock like a spirit returning to earth
or rather leaving it
as figures leave the shops to pattern wet streets
speaking for all of them in autumn
as time consumes itself in our society
and we consume its exile in our hearts

FAR AND AWAY

The fault mine
in lifted air caught in midday
impermeable behind the eye
like a page missing
to enforce a lie

or a man writing letters for work
banging against the door
against cold within a thing to hold
and hold, as pretty as gold
just lying about every day

thorns and wire make a last ditch pretty
cast shadows on nodules of flint

jaded light approaches cancellation
the desire of the mouth for the scar

No Resolution

Hold fast to
fast as
the changing sky

my square of window
changes shape
as if my eyes could fly

living on the edge of
hearing from you
under the same clouds

gentlest democracy
how hard you are
like a simple truth dismissed

The Night The

April 15/22 1986

bark abandoned on the night air
a distant recension by small creatures in a ditch
and an owl's crisp echo by the library

∾

some
people are sleeping
mouths fused by indifference
and blank tickets to symbolic realms

∾

mendacity?

∾

stocks rise
shuttered primroses
by the ground
ignore the commander-in-chief

∾

some things never sleep
it's the TV counterpart
you hear too much about
in other terms

∾

dead stone writers speak to ears of corn
and cloudbanks over Suffolk
and all that necessary oil
in the air

~

before first light
leaden with cultural determinism
breaks as self-defence
on a million radios
morally refuelled wakefulness
takes many forms
and we are all possessed.

Postcards to Spain 1986

1. A Note on Air and Motives

As unexplained for the most part
mere melody revolves in loops
of class and cloud: yet persons sing in pain

and wonder at their lives out loud.
This was the basis of so much, motive
even, and absorbed a great deal of attention

against which, for example, there was the swelling
sound of the Thälmann Brigade singing
as they marched. It cheered some people up.

Listen, don't worry, even about rust
and bills; it's a sharp possibility
that anything human may change

and the edge of song may be a razor
or a hedge of song erasing
unwanted lines of music from ordinary vistas.

2. CODA

That was a brigade of men.
There were no women in it
in that version of a war
as often happened.
However, women are not the meat in a vegetarian diet.

3. POINT BLANK FUTURE

The same day the wall cracked as if it was a sign of life
the same day was a voice in the air, falling quietly
the same day was a petition obscuring its intention
the same day I opened a tin and it was full of tiny marching
    children
the same day you spoke for hours I think
the same day hung over us all in clouds like blankets
the same day the meaning of marble escaped us
the same day was a voice in the dark
the same day I discovered necessity they killed Lorca
the same day is never unspoken unless by imaginary beings
the same day they were all *voluntarios de la vida*
the same day I went I came back
the same day abandoned by olive-green water
the same day shook with anger every time I passed it
the same day was a sudden tremor in the dry ground
the same day is a ghost of itself that you just catch a glimpse of
the same day is actually the fabric of society
the same day gazes out of your eyes as gazes out of mine
the same day we look and see arching or should that be
    searching?
the same day may not be what we want to be in this
the same day is the song that never rose from a million throats
the same day is not final, not the last word
the same day rings all day like a telephone
the same day won't call you, dear proletariat
the same day was the voice of an unwritten stone

4. WISH YOU WERE HERE

Imagine a band of fire to play
grey-blue clouds across an early death
in streets where any number of hearts waltz
in careless love, loving the emergent leaf
and smoking visions, the atmosphere
of May
    and who wouldn't leave it
for the tingling blade of a word or two
from you. Who would? As the venomous jets
that bind our ears
and the radioactive wind that softly sweeps
to a statement blind to the depths of balding sorrow
cement the justified moment
like revolving futures in a matte shot
from an open door

Take it again from here: my life rioted
at the light of dawn in my pocket, at the phrase,
at the overtime chorus of the fertile land
as it stops for the shout of Spain
whatever that was
on a train in the night
as it holds the wheel from inside
my spinning mouth, my Huesca, my Molesworth,
my comparisons, my bases in the altered light
of the world's outpouring!

Oh corn and guest and bell and summer field
if you should ever turn up again
feel free to stand by the vanished English line
till an operator gives you the international exchange
and you get through and hear the dazed clicks
of an integrated system on a life-support machine.

Postcard to Italy

At times the land's edge whitens into tidal debris
lolling under the early light
as relenting curves of sleep suck at the pebbles

and shards of warbling dream are suddenly revealed
fading into sand in case the rational grasp
turns over too heavily into an old injury

such as memory could be made out to be until the full light
screens the olive trees inland by the moment
and cars drive fast down all the curvy roads

establishing daytime tracks beside the longing grasses,
the reading knowledge of a language.
I think here I am not making music like the faithful cuckoo

among the alien streets lit by yesterday's trading figures
ne l'ora che comincia I tristi lai
la rondinella presso a la mattina . . .

That shadow that I was asleep shortens into the day
I hope to have: absence hanging like the amber warmth
of a sun across my path to provide a note of laconic solvency

as I shave. The thought of your face fills the glass
at once like heat echoing on a red hillside
to dance over the silvering like a deceptive vision

or erase a wind solo rising like smoke to disperse
night before I want it to, water in the basin clouding
as the day will here, later, as the air thickens in token.

A Reading

Silvered glass. Approach a person. Hover in thought.
Flick at the catch, stammer in Gerrman,
about the burning sky and its helmsman
in dead shadow.

      It was a flame between each finger
in every heart that heard her words,
a memory of the structure of the 'as'.

The further glass stands unframed still
against the columns, the image unopened,
being little more than it ever was, but there
to care about the desperate calm
and virtual person lying in the light.

L'Histoire

Flames cloy the traverse
work appeals for
means by
a silence
inside each egg of day
would venture out
with a shawl
from beside the self
towering against a prison
like an azure poison
pinned across the right
by the right of way

It was one voice
they spoke with
don't tell me
they were poor
they danced
& used to tiptoe
by the prison
when the moon was red
like a fated harvest
curling in the air.

Small Changes

As fades the tractor homeward
and folded day tilts
to a vacant field and beams
from the image of a house

So colour returns to a small
refugee moon
and a musical evening begins
downing a quick one

Before the glass reveals
a remodelled nose, and from the mouth
if a voice then a voice
of exacter pitch

On such tethered scale
the music burns up
in a classic image
of third-world melancholia

What the eye can't see
in a fanciful sieve
of starry empathy
won't do no good my dear

Unflapped pastoral maybe
let slip or caught
by a bow incomplete then
under the arc of charity.

Guinea on China

Don't let spaces, budding lines,
drop cracked on the red margin.
The isle of plenty is a communal dream
but not if, don't forget, the cost is
not too much soft leather.

In the bar, salty saucers, how dated
zinc would be! Take a computer, bad head,
in low gears after the missile trailer
winking red. Go home and go to bed.
The last wore out the question
beneath the misty moon.

Don't turn your back on animal faces
I took him to mean. There's no sense
in the original. Green folder, I love you
as webs drift on whitewash. Reform.
I never heard so much lost breath.

High Time

Light breaks windows
cats shiver
road works wink
in a steady consensus
hurting like a necklace
set press to wear it
and pass into the opera
radiant gabble
saying nothing personal
at breakfast
in the course of true love
a first course in not dying
or going mad
in the shops
so bipolar activity leads to
a short and happy clasp
such as we can feel
at the back of the neck
to transcribe this shining information
as it comes
in spite of the clear tide
years peak out
the ruffled sand flattens
and a misty line
of rust unseals a touch
of friendly eye-contact
and keeps going
like a voice on the line
I want to hear occasionally
to be hit in the brain
as the day comes back
we all do, we need this
text of memory
renewed by radiant states

flagged and reflagged in new growth
from low on the imperial stem
for all the shadowy exercises
in the nocturnal mirror
of another power we watch
newspaper pasted
over our eyes.

The First Intervention

Last light floats past the black trees.
Another dollar. A great bill and a force
for change. It definitely falls to one another

to read Russian, to say nothing of this
kindly moment or that. Surfacing between my teeth
it felt like a language, a bitter phone

you love to use in slow motion curtain,
that love reconstituted in blue on blue
as our capital sells its skin for time out of mind

and sustains us on the edge of talk, grey,
absent or annulled to the core
streaming out loud across the entire space.

WHEN IT SEEMED THAT ALL WAS LOST

Some sleeping head reclining in a different spirit
dreams in amber and glass against all time to come
eyes closed to the kind flux of light and likeness.

The light cuts hard buildings around us, shadow
conniving with sweet rhythms and hot food to shape
ideologies, snapped and dotted into every heart.

So the dearest future creatures beneath the sun, set down and
        loved with a purpose
to outrun any fingered lapels on a light-weight suit
imagined the scene and ran it, hiding behind newspapers in a
        small café

Where a new journey was a defined shadow on the driest
        martini
like the light of tyranny sharply bleeding off earlier
        contemplation
poured back so the mask keeps its humane appearance.

What we would buy is gone deep within us like a hanging
        thought
and projected like an old dove on to our silly retinas
in a fashionable curtain print to keep the world at bay

While pudgy fingers deal in sleep futures on a grand scale
and the time is destitute because it lacks the web of names it is
and how it is concealed and revealed in trafficking those coins.

The sleeping body turns at this point, muttering words
from the communards, advertising financial services buttered
        up for the taking
and sleeps on in darkness, for all the world like a quietened
        bestowal.

Solo

Basal options are deleted by the things
he done and how they could never augment
kindly note and burn the novel, like indoor fireworks
extruding weightless narrative as it goes up
in smoke. The rest is doing us good on the cards
so they introduce a policy review for clustered
antipathy and idleness promising crisp vision
tomorrow. But it's not a matter of luck
they've screened such humdrum cries out at the terminal
to reduce shock at the new South East, it's
dead behavioural, ministers lying there in white
parole. Hearing voices is getting commonplace.
The shot tower was one refuge from reaching hands
though the smell was no way smart, not with the sun
up there all day. Solo wants help. Pages and pages
of typescript under grey ash, can you hold
or call again thrice on the social fund.
At times argot shows through brittle speechifying
to release a little comfort for the papers, attacks the heart
casually and tosses it into ragged robin. Then
the spectacle continues an attractive prospect
and at the same time avoids payment.
The delegation walked right through a strip search
like they had bags on their heads,
on soft leather; pink hands clutch the option
to develop, as a matter of crafty units
chained to the day like lunch. A researcher did the writing
and it dissolved all memory, till the white bodies
lay at the subway entrance, or rocked on their stumps,
completed bandaged in the quiet light. Canvas
stories hang and defy vision in a virtual flick
of his head on the button as if it was ever so. Solo refuses sleep
and spreads over the land on automatic drill,
a virtual factor, chalking on the odd wall of death.

Wherever a Head

Wherever a head appears through flesh in a glassy extrusion of
     fond
ignorance svelte with immaculate novelty and covered against
     weeping,
to find something crackly at the fingers' end would be a polity
in miniature, some hyperbolic but dark-suited absence stepping
     down
from an official car and its sheeny populist vision.

On the other head be it, the official crown of weeds and old
     mortar
running down to the nape where the old dream convulses in
     lung disease
sucking the pebbles back in the throat as the dated tidal
lyric stemmed by sun voting predictions takes its place in every
bedside anthology of lost or executed souls.

This eye bedizened with puzzling, what can you expect? Such
     random
stock hammered deep into the lease creates a loud humming
     across
pretty plastic tables, such perfect teeth scavenging the burger
for hot pickle traces, when they do lie too much for tears
glistening on poppy and meadowsweet stalks the headlines say.

For what they say is equally the case and thus flares up
from day to day. Habit. Imagine there are four movements in all
and practise them in several languages. What would there be to
     love
most? Heavens above, I don't need to tell you how to long
for absent social beauty. He was a lovely entertaining speaker.

Deep end days and nights have their stars and blotto vagaries
from one word to the next she says holding well on a wet surface
but might as well have trusted to luck. No time was so oiled
or palm lines so believed or so run by martial options.
They cut the price, you see, and just loved the issue.

Returning to black and white a screen flickers over the sea
and we listen to a story that there is neither we nor I in
so the sentences are ploughed back leaving arms under the
          sodden
soil belt. Slender chance called upon steps lightly under the rain
and the most pitiful stumps beckon and sprawl perversely.

Fear might abate the volume of attentive imagery in a flurry of
          paste
on the tongue. All I could hear was some state of being
but it's good to have ears at all. The air is full of water.
Grooves and cavities inspire language from street to street
as they always did, body and paper, as light goes on and off.

The Name of Day

You pay to go in, you act
on information
and to break the ice you die
a hero. Block the door
if you are so anxious
as an attic charm
from the dead
and unscripted returns
through all eternity
in an eyebrow.

Teeth flush to china
bats cavort and rise again
& fade on wings of thought
because of the mirror.
It fails the sense, becomes
inert and brushed as light on a pebble
wet by sea or rain.

No state to be in
like blue lines
on the willow scar by the pipes
coming together in a shelly wetland
courtly song and dance.
We don't amount to nothing
like the movies' sacred finery,
the blinder blindness of a phrase
about a day in my pleasant land
specked with fragments
of strategy in a ditch.

There's more to fear where this comes from.

Say Nothing

Envied light
glittery leaf
flatten out
disordered hope

nettle words
on all my skin
black water
can't quite hear

a virtual grid
frames each gust
billows inward
in sudden grey

take out the bone
to play down
fallen webs
of local acts

arrange trees
in binding twain
by clock time
set fast

no rash act
as symptom
simply nothing
bears renewal

we are in line
to shadow falls
of will, we owe
more than it says.

Section Three 1991–2002

Sestina

Autumn as chill as rising water laps
and files us away under former stuff
thinly disguised and thrown up on a screen;
one turn of the key lifts a brass tumbler—
another disaster probably averted, just,
while the cadence drifts in dark and old.

Voices of authority are burning an old
car on the cobbles, hands on their laps,
as if there was a life where just
men slept and didn't strut their stuff
on stage. I reach out for the tumbler
and pour half a pint behind the screen.

The whole body is in pieces. Screen
memories are not always as sharp as old
noir phenomena. The child is like a tumbler
doing back-flips out of mothers' laps
into all that dark sexual stuff
permanently hurt that nothing is just.

I'm telling you this just
because I dream of watching you behind a screen
taking your clothes off for me: the stuff
of dreams, of course. Tell me the old, old
story, real and forgetful. Time simply laps
us up, like milk from a broken tumbler.

A silent figure on the stage, the tumbler
stands, leaps and twists. He's just
a figure of speech that won't collapse
like the march of time and the silver screen;
like Max Wall finally revealing he was old
and then starting again in that Beckett stuff.

I'd like to take my sense of the real and stuff
it. There's a kind of pigeon called a tumbler
that turns over backwards as it flies, old
and having fun; sometimes I think that's just
what I want to do, but I can't cut or screen
out the lucid drift of memory that laps

my brittle attention just off-screen
away from the comfortable laps and the velvety stuff
I spilled a tumbler of milk over before I was old.

Tense Fodder

Nous n'avons pas une voix seulement pour parler, mais aussi
pour faire silence.
JEAN-LOUIS CHRÉTIEN

THE GARDEN PARTY

Committed to daylight did this to me
used it to poison air water and the soil

no heroism or bomb-throwing
just objects recurring in modified modes

green as any known idle reverie
questions are recorked for tomorrow's sacrifice

original skin hums as if to extend
me against a different background

writing in the border with an inky pen
no scent of marjoram, no arbiter of time

these shadowy English beds exploit hope
to preserve value and misery and no alternative

is silent in the will of shade where fathers
hammer vocabulary to induce dreams of purpose

going for broke in some ludicrous home
putting a distant hand in the transparent air.

Hide the tree, conceal personal distress
wear and take off clothes in a blind bracket

and vanish as I speak. I can't understand strangers
but they're the somatic death I'm travelling into

After I've gone don't fizzle out drinking bottles
in the shower that falls from the unbreathed sky

write or cut shades of my name in the bark
and ring retraction with a hard colloid edge.

No Contact

Think of the dark falling too much and be angry, some reflex
incentive and they sit back and do nothing in a lather

killing a few for the cameras but the red sand and the rocks
fade as the air heats up and slithers out of the shade.

Bare voices. Not even mine
probably off the radio talking about the economy

ringing in the new light grey layers of ash
and future shape of blarneying puppetry

I can hardly call it waste or political aesthetic
or shopping around like blood in vacancy

armed with psychotic birds gaping
and gasping for derivation, it's gone

here and now and forever. No cut, no finish
recursive ink narrating a single case, a recent case.

What did he do? I'll tell you what he did
or hindered even a few flowers and their sweetness and troubles.

How some casual reach bludgeoned the mouth
for want of an intenser care

and the dazed function of colour
just bled off into unrectified threads

blown about by the breath of a few words.

A want of all the virtues had remained intact
as the airport or the market

sniping at fish and coffee in their safe little
corridors of grief and promising days of late spring

attended by a vast audience, all unmoved. I thought
something else once in a European country, watching the
  almond tree.

Some fathers, some mothers, given up in a circle
for a kinder pain, hate these keen objects

and their lazier dreams of substitution
in case of pulling the strings alike

and even cry generously for another aptitude to a name
but what can they buy for a betrayed ornament?

Punish a few, kill a few and wade back out of the shallows
cradling a fish. Is that so cruel?

You could call it the national question after all
and beg it to stop. You could call it her wish for a child.

A slow drip or a ripple of severity
striating naked backs in the treasury

smothered each smile in blindness,
figured the stupid, and I didn't notice.

Walking in the streets openly
I have no-one to blame but myself

and still fail to vanish. What you call
an ignoble world is an open question.

The planes fly low over the present trappings
and fade loudly away. No contact.

Another concealed entity of restless embargo
has disinfected a far landscape

if we can decipher the dots properly.
This effigy is speaking again

and signs of resistance leak into the air.
There is an exceptional glow fuelling it.

These Days

Flat out on a council argument
lost as a pencil, guarded as a résumé

it's true it was nothing deep
just a person in trousers

moments of a life swoop
even eat out of her hand

crumbs of mental storm
played twice in the same key

looking for the checkout
to classify some trace of being

more than being and less than anything
in green and blue ordinary life

swelling up and splitting for history
into a pair of opposites

my girlish heart rearranges
the long and the short

to prospect for all the lost boys
lugged through the meat

resources of entropy call my
bluff mannerisms to renounce

slow motion advertising conduits
of carnage by plastered lack

and then come back and fall to the ground
at the frontiers the glass

areas of time full of implicit
regret for designated readings

and still hoping for a moment
of street light to shape

odd words into sentences suspended
until written down the side

of stung and planted ground
from the homeless feet up

to the vast mouth it crams
with nobody's utopian shadows

obviously needing credit
from time to time.

THE WIRE

Crueller ones all hearts enchaining
sit under a tree in the afternoon

wondering what to obey. Internally
they are us in the currents

that sweep us into the idea
of years of paid labour

slipping into pockets
in regard to sex for example

photographing streets
in unconscious investigations of painting

all surfaces sheened by the rain
on a winter evening

bumping against light skies
wanting the impossible illness

this idiot revenge strokes
my face and wipes away my hope

a fine collusion sets store by
any rate it can get

divided by and thus creates
a world of awkward mental life

pending imagined faults
against some indifference

beneath revolving painted air
my little brother, my son,

my unattained and certain boundaries
emitted as quasi-military release

from torn or flashing want
to be at hand as bright as an adept gaze

at local deaths blinkered
by dancing fires

mythic amplitude trapped in a wire
certainty of tumbling dusk

as if my life depended on it.

LESS AND LESS

What you haven't got I imagine
hollowed out like in a fever

in mist over ploughed fields
we saw something on the bench bound up

making it a figure with notes
suggestive of committal

circles behind the coarse effect
making a noise like speech

a gestalt image deflects the camera
arrangement from the normal window

such a surprise the last object
promptly brought a reminder

for poorer states and regions
where the mother's life was rejected

only to be expressed as a joke
along the railway line

colour was cut from magazines
with a residuum of death

their value may increase in Africa
but to have a heart

I have to be in pain or separation
distance varying in length

from different linguistic desire
and spilled coffee

half a life continuing the social poetry
she called them tributes

to the rhythmic shadows of
the very act of this world

and I call it a game with sticks
by grasping it and any system

to make sense without end
a possible world war

like some sort of bank
for intersubjective transactions

I'm certain it was a field
with tinned food and stunted trees

everyone knows what to do
when they go crazy

they write a long digressive poem
on the balcony and wait for trains

hurtling through loss of interest
to quote at some length from local usage

resting by the fiercest negatives
to help cope with the same time

in the midst of thick columns of smoke
and leaving matters at that.

SLEEP

Looking for it. What I absorb from a bank
is meaning something I don't want to like
and need to love outside the borrowed life
to be worked off and forgive and forget.

If I knew what the absence was it would be
orange against the grass in the rain. Yes
and too heavy to lift, reserved for us,
a vision passed on, a sum to expect.

Not there. No story. Ingesting something
eight years old during the night
looking for some doorway into the dark
my balance has o'erstepped my will

and nettles catch my skin instead of
fair outlook switchback nausea
projects the outside of buildings
in the same recursive pattern over development plans

longer and longer shadows search abroad
for what I love I forget to light,
what being proper stories hates to be
will not be refunded.

The cubists painted other fronts too
leaving the bill as nature, looking sweet
inside a monument to eating in public
and arrested investigators of fraud

for fraud in the story still looking for
something good in the story of the resistance
of glass to stone as the outer ripple
eats the rest like a photocopier.

THIS AND THAT

From that time onwards I believed
a small painting of a subject
flung back what the silence wished
and did not obtain

For years I lived in common with it
and spines on shelves
welling up like a kind of milk
which it does not matter

In terms of interchange I was
a few steps down the street and back
in a denim jacket for my given body
a hard and fast label is the thing

Which of course the phone confirms
and shrouds me over and poisons
life all night in case of technology
all right rhetoric

Dreaming full of live weight
of conviction that instates the realm
looked out through glass at the
full moan of the singing air

Unwise to walk by
or gloss the muddiness of words
once in existence
shifting by dint of surprise

I'd come and go at any price
but I'm beyond it:
then it rains then stops and
then the blackbirds again.

What will warn us of our disposal?
certainly not prose or bits of paper
photocopies piled up and stapled
and doubtless more arduous etc.

Who writes something new
that sets no limits
to dwelling or dawning
or telling or mourning

Painfully sewn in complete
silence made visible
by small holes in the folds
between this and what it says.

Lino Cut

So many mothers haul the fat engine of day
up the shaft and cook the awful flesh

letting go some corporate intuition of our history
sits ill on a flawed window sill

and still a stubble-faced memory burns
spades and suddenly attacks the newspaper

stokes the columns for a war
and brings the geraniums in for movement

a thinking red. Go or go. Did you find
acid pain on what page? Each leaf curls as I think

so I don't feel no pain in the dark
but I don't breathe symbols anyone can hope

to nearly cluster over the usual London spot
in a box, how can you be so kind?

I try to read another person's words
wood lip round time chamfered for safety

only pines bound to a short life among courted
sentences from San Diego to anywhere else you like

tell their own story and won't be some purge
in material death, no more quick dance

to tell you the shift in space is all
there is if you want us to continue the search.

A BIT APART

Vanity and clumsiness will not be lyric
fodder as they inhere or blaze forth

just qualities in the mutagenic pall
breathed in by mothers with shut windows

and long strokes of grey bestowing politics
like a management buy-out of the Habsburgs

the grey veers into push-button metaphor
an effective strategy review for the eastern outlook

(in Chancellor Kohl's punitive liberation
Arbeitslosigkeit macht frei)

modelling provides a new point of view for the imaginary
a harlequinade of futures in black and white

it disintegrates before our eyes
described as a glaring example of the gulf between

hope and hold, always setting one against it
or making representations (if I thought

how could a mountain be secret? if space shrinks
so much won't the words conspire?)

but looking across the chemical works from this sealed window
at the lank birds dropping like dandruff

I think they are representing loss of speech.

LOOK BACK

How poplars froze crisply
against the light. Orange.

Observers don't lift fingers.
To lips. A sticky idealism

over a vista of nice times.
Watch as you curl up inside

with a story made to a formula
of natural matters.

Only on completion of the news
from tiptoe to freedom as more news

in fact as the truth came
though shot at willingly.

Now that it's warmer you can take
a jersey off without lucky prices

on the books that look so new
and yet without which it is not sustained.

When I move my eyes
the upheaval is apparent

these are my several fields
the path lies under them, intense

and hazy under frost or columbine.
History never abandons itself.

FACING PAGE

Vision unrolls vertically
based on a sphere pressed flat at meeting

looking ahead to a time
to offer dispersed meanings

well coded construction rates
a strange list of comfort

visible in country of origin
as local expenditure buds

cutting loot from right to left
long past nightfall

masks in the stash
in body order face oblivion

with his mother tongue
his most fluent encounter with money

a literal beginning in the eyes
of bright green cultural property

so little or no vestige
cut to an honorary degree

to the dealer behind the writer
be sure of a concealed hand

wash out your ears if you want
to set foot in the same door

your skin a hostage to bits of dust
from life still to come

healing slowly away
met off a stopping train after Royston

everything can end in songs
filling mouths with torn work

shed as piecemeal calm by terms
you dare not touch in the morning

or observe the slight figures
driven into a corner by blood and language

open to visitors *au plan juridique*
clustered gaze on the hoardings

still no sign of resistance to
the taste of food destroying its name

you can get it in tiny orange threads
called linkage. Why not be day-neutral?

No need for a spoke in the right
moment called the end

if I can so express it
called a cover version of fission

a floating glass threshold
leaves the enclave without sleep

anyone who cares to take a white powder
can write the first two acts

or a tender scene with a bit of time
slipping into a crude mark appraisal

the shadow of the press text
obscures the title

tense before and after death
in the eventual play of hungry roots

sell starry gaps between illusions
of a service economy and backwash

refuse to stick with plausible sedatives
so the dog only confirms the limit

the loss is absolute from several habitats
not just in the sky

an illegible privacy set up all over Europe
in a fine type of public disgust

believing in objects
is deranged

turn to page seven
for the photo of another face.

DRYING OUT

More about spoke down nothing but
nice in dust and despatches

my homily moments on the wheel
fined each of them twenty pounds

on the spot. These daft sequels
sang bravely, heaved over the wall

round the spine, badly afraid of
dying out of all proportion to the light

forms of reversal into sponge. What the day
brings forth as image of the past homage

fades at once, threshold of general satisfaction
in the plan of the central station

call it what you will, pronounced
shudder. Petit-bourgeois red meat fanciers

with their ways of life adored the
scattered flakes of cloud cover

miners and all who set out the same camp
come down to a breath of orange

without title, sex or character
revised since above, free as the rabbits

of the garrigue underfoot, storms
abridged attempting to be substantial

zero I for another glass please
but read hopscotch in the works of time

that final window an emblem on the pavement
is brought home to any imaginary weapon

legal web for certain powers of real food
split open and vomiting fine dust

over the table. Moscow print washes out
as if accidentally faced in order

the relief drum a dedicated thing to die of
any time you see it. Now you don't.

New York

Touched by a lifetime
response left like a cloud
in her eye as yet buried

last number recall buttons
tendered and the connection
doesn't want to pay for

what you know anyway
she is smiling on the subway
in about 1958, at night

called a sheaf of young writers
quasi una shadow crossed
precisely at three thirty

marked by writing perhaps
until it was finished, and even then.

Some Title

Basic flame stands in yellow fog as copse
or corpse logging functions in the distance
of the general earth, a charred mill stands
out of narrow time roundly offered over
dim followers at war with the faces often
recognised. Stake ripped in the heart of
us, from elders on, or a blind or a lamp dew
on grass flickering to dying out can only re-
cord what it won't forget until after a sleep.

Come over all the bridge nightingales, go
for the acorn hue, jeopardise thrill to a dull
ochre. Drop infancy holdings from another
long night of vertiginous collapse, give her
a renewed taste for life and tidy up and cook it.
Clean the primal stove, looking up. Opt
for thinking under grids and over tasty this
and that function as if, say, a stone to be pro-
nounced or put in the way of how it turns out.

In another naughty hit a couched delphic feeling
does not transform any animal in a letter
to thy hart. The jug, the bowl, the impasto
is my retyred minde, you find it out at a long
laugh scorning all the cares of famine, fabric
choice driven from skies and hedges into normal
bin end searches for even a lark. Say what you
hear, the light has gone and detach and expel
take their place as überwords conjoined to us.

Let me put this out. Though roses flag and dip
in dark memory, stress disrupts their prosody
from one to the other and ever back again in
September, where dash is tied down to handle
with care, or if you wish and drop suddenly
out of sight, death. Set this to come and go and
swallow it down until it clips a lie like a peppery
olive rises in a mother clasp, all grist and iris
dresses. If it's old enough I'll pay to have it, truly.

I'll pray to have it, to make it clear within, and
contained with a mind to match. At the start of
this clue what but pain? Kingfishers for mental
concept of growth as opposed to even moral
sex in a chair, as he would say, how sad after the
reading yet another transformation of the part.
Pinch is destroyed, warm feelings, colour gummed
up and over views of treacly Sunday dissent. Go
down and see, answer the door, step after step.

Drawn by the very worst for what? Wear? Huddle
of erosion may help as if listening also describes
a frame of open doors and windows, if there is a
sense of movement perhaps even found to matter.
Kelp bed and west wind, cries of a pen in various
ways of treating me just kind of melt the flora of
exile. Play is implored by the bank whereon the time
expires in Latin letters, the break comes naturally
if the ringing is exact enough to grow on the shore.

Much More Pronounced

The enigma [of depth] consists in the fact that I see things, each one
  in its place, precisely because they eclipse one another, and that
  they are rivals before my sight because each one is in its own place.
                                                    M. MERLEAU-PONTY

It is, after all, our very uncertainty about their seriousness that
  makes it possible for ghosts to continue to affect us.
                                                    JONATHAN ELMER

Don't we really want
the cranks of nine
black cap of piquant set
in little ivory sombrero
at my wit's end?

Here we have radiant doll
in an old bag of ready catch
mellow bead wrist to pull
with wired devotion
as her screen image

I didn't like to look
out of it, slogan treated as
it is wonderful to hear
all tricked up and vapid
and acclaimed our censors said

Or didn't we? Slice trivial
squeaks of nations, reel times
buzz off arid and plain
holding a weapon in each
other art and rock with mirth

Really bottled England of twin
prophets by some ironic past
served a slim ordeal
as a sort of temple so I say
yes to her rag arms of refuge

A moth and the knife boy
want stone about to step
forward for many of us
earlier the being masks
father wakes the point of it

To be ripped off with compliments
for the soul and made the outer
sound whistles and gasps
comprehend the crowds that look
over an art occupation

Like the task whose task is
all the other dead once more
augurs of this change will speak
the stones and our conceptions, yes
as a lip to scrap our witty person

A double fatal ground
owns life in other words
an exaltation we call love
for the person bearing it stumbling
about a panic pot label

His or mine? In the name
of the mistake
a question arises
alive in a split power hand
wrapped about that decadent thought

The best we can be under the sky
new data for a long negation
made from bad shape
natter on song and larval address
so get it down on real paper

What is to be dead? You get back
all residence on earth
and row me over a charmed life
you want to go somewhere
crowd to the front of the stage

Little red rooster refuse to plague
relics in a ruin of glass
hardly a definite proposal
fresh wind blowing fond of the state
and a little wine dry as a bone

The lake is wonderfully sad and quiet
black water as still as death
I have your kind note
there is nothing for it
as much as I like to hear

The catch is the voice run
on hypnotic images or
dolls on a plane if the ticket
to inner vision in a suave
nut-shell seemed wanting

A wish to indicate we can
bleach abstract thought to a dot
may invent details (he is
depressed, I was afraid of this) both
in an imperfect replica

Competing species of plant life
revamp urban fire drill
get more than they pay for
uncase pressure from below
and fly in the face of art

Only the French and Chinese
cure in the brine waves
the obstacles being removed
in a golden fashion
and held in this light bowl

Having to be distant
he began a more complete account
for dust, damp, soot, mice and worms
when it was packed away
to do this till he was dead

Survivors of a family
if they mastered the emptiness
during the filming of this chance
yes I do understand your
untold stories that lie behind it

Cellophane heart I'm talking to
you and poetry after making your order
you won't hear from us
the best ways to use each one
come to those who wait

Hanging over our heads
a withering flash due to
regret cannot be renewed
blind as a battered case
of ever their mother had thought

Another shell cracks in helpful
pain drizzled with oil
and smeared with saline
solutions not to be had except
by the present itself

Unspeakable fair this silence
haunts me thus with feare
so I'm writing to tell you
miles before it's gone
in exchange for a living wager

A slightly open black gate
objectively new and yellow
a topaz mist going up like a shutter
to disclose too much acidity
coming now to hang on

To be rescued alone to advertise
writing to drive and drive
and end up with a life of bewildered
autobiography in muffled fabric
O baby what allure to a changing face!

I should ascribe the boundaries
of this country to awe
and eye to steeple
at a point where its sudden balm
slips off and is visibly enacted

Isn't it time that we were familiar with
the ultimate purpose of humanity?
Flowers, sea-shells, answers and chains,
artfully carved birds on the branches of trees,
what do poets praise more highly?

Nothing stops awash with blood
real fast as an egg. Post me it
to be what there is in the process
of it flavoured by trains
and their evocative night calls

Nothing but time to any of these
cold stars properties as questions
know that I'll want patents of
how life ought to be lived at night
thrown away like a country gesture

Shocks as fatal as toasting soap
a man poured and set over
windy ramparts thou art blind
as sheep at last your nape
in the clouds ajam with scudding

Fishing in sleep furniture
torrents of outer rafters
buy me lines mate and foam
boogy-woogy abstracts
in order to order this

A passage lamp somewhere else
faithful to that epoch
the journal jerks the strings of
scarf or socks or rags of time
to repair the grammar of music

So drive on past daffodils
made in the open mouth
in ink for the future
leaving it to the mercy of
my own fate my hand

Writing to remain alive as
something emptied into time
the balcony was something else
dyed in the wool of an awkward self
like a blue stain on stucco reason

Such white tunes burn
like nobody's business only
brackets hold us up here
and European languages spill out
of every literal appearance

To see or lapse into a happier state
was the art of the circus
all lucky legs and camels
to bring you satisfaction
or your money back

The fathers could then be
recomposed diegetically to
form a cycle or shared meaning
compatible with a system of
discounting by arguing too much

Not being able to crumple
as a block when things get difficult
information requires amendment
I would be grateful if you could
let me know this as soon as possible

At night the joint fears minimum
tales of backstreet tariff ways
to request a value for money
or tiptoe like trees along
the canal miles from the market

By accident her arm grew
darker than the future was
because they had no choice with
great anxiety flavoured with salt
as a prime exchange paradigm

She thought the answers were slight
objects like lapis allergies shackled
to first return of a mother's terror
hiding her peak intonation as
functions that fate has dealt us all

Beginning at five not in fact Jewish
edges of the sea should invite distaste
at the printed words coalition
of clustered or prickly scraps of landscape
to loop evenly up covering the shells

So it was voice mainly as despatches
from the given waves of serotonin
in a continual buzz of self leakage
on to deterrent maxims waved about
flat-out remedies for denying anything

Gleaming above the porch the idea
of providing a floor battled the moths
in grim theory shadowed by Schutzbund
fantasies and weakened by two fungal
growths and a new corporate logo

If such a new dome of time
and transparent distance wraps
it all up with a compressed attachment
quickly take up a corn-flower
or hop to the darker shadow glitch

The eye and a pure delight in the
topics piece and slip forced from the sea
to be shot and stuffed for academic
frisson but on balance a fear of being
alone would say its images bluntly

Suppose her her head positive
but even more simple reader
the spectacle I might be too weak
not chic these dared to hope for
turns new moral access of heroic size

This forthright dream is style
at your feet in dayglo fronds and
speaks vivid walls confronting the
old traces to adorn the wolf
days unless you'd rather not

The white bear drifting across
the chain of her grandfather
like a winsome speedwell
might nominate the time of
aspen betrayal that we show

And cash it in without
hyperbole or incompletion
just at the edge of salt objects
under the tongue
sucking the Labour Party Manifesto

And so lash will to substance
at the bar impending some
diffusive wrack of silk
bother against massy clouds
and farewell strips of tissue

How can you talk like that?
phantom trio of early life
sleep in some coddled past
look back at the target fish
swept up in tragic kitchen practices

Listen to the rhythm of the
forming raid on the inartistic
cloths of grief: charred entities
laid neatly out, their lines
bundled into a noise of weeping

Feel little or nothing of the cause
my sole thought, watch the birdie
eat the lamb by the fell. By
the fallen understand
nothing but black and more black

Mother tongue plight in short
change is solid and durable
the dolly in the copper
a surprise to the memory
like a line of wet battery jars

Step up to my second question
in tangible words such as
what is the chance of
asking how you could say
something like that

A late afternoon myth
tangles in the entity's small flame
mouth open in sudden death
and fair lines. Used to
is a defective verb

Novel thought is too long
gone to be netted
I now realise and what resembles
analogy is layered in passing
time to its other domain

It's all anaphora now
threatening the system. Can't you
see it again and combine the terms
in a veranda with a view to
an outcome by autumnal beeches?

Pruning leaves traces that grow
semantically past first in a
version of democracy. A grid
underlies as what lies outside
growing up through it would if it could

Some secret agency passes for time
if the same applies to words
with only a slight thickening
in the black cap experienced
as a bitter maxim about standards

To collapse is not enough
to die from the same coin:
the same system to defeat itself
falls sharply as winter comes on
in an imaginary landscape

Piquant screen time on a light
breeze stay on the other hand
go out of this body
effracted into endless
bavardage instead of seeking

Which raises instruments of a
concrete whistle and does
eventually speak out
good visions in the air
so that this turns proverbial

Feet on the ground glass turn
and run for a hefted lark
as when to outstrip occult
funny business would turn heads
in true and in trim filade

Less than that time for
food cannot displease any man
burned up across the water
until all of animated nature
is as good a tactic as not at all

Across the plain a proleptic
cascade remains to be seen
under patches of reddening
light and carpathian distances
the wine is thin and confected

Spatial memory-traces of the
timing of tactile stimuli make
cortical maps that precipitate
more internal wilderness when
the whole array is moving

Why on earth is a serious
thing and the chalk-lines
closer rippled or ready to
come and hallucinate it
pronounced unspeakable

Maintained my grip like a leaf
out of time or perhaps
visionary for detail in our
matrix to complete the trope
say a rift in the irony map

Of course a cap on the cable
is not the same as culture when
we wrap a kind of puppeteer
bursting a history of this point
into that remarkable word amiss

Most men do not dislodge her
without some show trial
in terms of simple location
nomadism is a place of its own
acutest at its vanishing

Thus the snow will fall
while I am somewhere
listening to a cantata like so little
dark falling out of place
with the rest of wild being

Or asleep in copper beeches
reduced to map the nether way
of detail so easily disowned
inscribed with acids
as the guarantor of the sky above

You call it psychology
a bit eager for a taste of words
again scampering about the attic
a slice of scumbled dreamwork
to complete my meaning

Did you ever think of one thing?
What is your own language?
Another glass in the silvery light
alternating in function between
funk and fiction, go on say it

Most of the time is at stake
for once between the lines of force
something blue branches out
when the phrase returns
singing loudly in both keys

Must we mourn what we say
the mother asks too little
the girl turns to her father his
consulting injury you will think
as I do is a reproach to light

In your writings refrain from
the organic world with one more train
of thought and threaten its taming
not a telepathic message but
the outcome would remain the same

How can we bring this penis
to the fire? or cash the panic
scorn food too much in Italian
verse forms braided tressed and
underwritten in this very room

Believe me the wild place-name
is held to account for me
atop black days for the index
curls up in the cold dreams
with further precipitation in sight

Her screen image only survives
in his sleeping arm my wood
is polished wood and gleams
by the nesting-box of a long
translation from the other past

It is moving what I write
against the odds the heart
of the wheel unties the line
like a wake for a vast conjecture
on the natural production of concepts

Parts of sleep when all is said
and done suggests much more
by the disclosure by an
intervention murmurs in the ear
what is actually perceived

If the far paradigm set fair
in the literal sense of
which he walks over the field
the small sound of wound
must entail a pair of authors

A filial snow against the
fence covers the ends of
lines in unspeakable notation
hard and fast rules at last
in a search for content

Thus the final stage is what
should fill its worst extreme
inner being from this inconstant
of the inner to a language
often speaking at the same time

Oh Snooty

for Ben Watson

Off the bone we swing down the street
heroic old figures full of stillness in
face of listless farewells and inky tropes
for thinking over. The cold blue sky is free
of smudges even if not simultaneously gassy
enough to breathe openly, caught at the
moment of birth in a circling whoosh of
extended caprice like molecules of national
emergence into a betrayal of all we once stood
for. Carry this for me while I count wave
after wave of sorry explanation, coming back
first class with stars in his eyes from an evening
of tacky piano fumblings and savage policy.
When I was younger I read the passage transcribed
above, and lost confidence in land, handed
back and put together with pipe-smoke point
of view about contracting pupils and mournful
time over the summer. It could equally well be
so now, if some version of it was playing
locally, quietly, round the corner. Between paintings
there is this wash deeper in brilliance
and may be already gone when you put it down
as his grief. A problem has happened
has been dedicated as I ask now at the end of
demanding more lifetime correspondence of our
health and our work. And indeed there was a job for him
although he kept on writing. The windows broke
and the army displays a genuine soul business
with bombs and rockets and madness and romance
like a stage advantage conscious of huge details
of a small lampshade which is present and mad enough
in a torture chamber coming round all the time
about to change back into song clatter.
Much more to grind is also the main individual

thing, in the comfort of his own guilt. In violence
on the new statute we replay the fifties among
the glasses, the dishes, the sofa, the story's remorse.
Don't elide the words, they mean everything to you.

Oh, To Be in England

What is this state if affection binds to shatter its
own suturing, if empty light throws up damages,
if stuttering vehicles pose as derivative maxims and admonitory
puzzles of blind restraint? How smart can these be?
The wooden surface belies substance, the soft cloth of
years deepening gloss to a pitch of narcissism
fluted bravely to clinging air. Catch it before it goes
too far, please deflect the ice topics, dead looks
bound by both types to deserve a figurative cool benevolence.
Oriental grounds leech the final vision for padding steps
down to two earlier pages, to form a cortical sale
eager to grow a second skin. She let fall a kind of remark. A
        spine
of no human place combining blue with whiter skin
failed to juggle with them in the dark fashions of conjugation,
attacked the children in a crowd of syrupy poisoners
bursting through the door for the sober results of an obscure
        fear.
Shock in its crudest liturgy would form a crust
on the pool surface, ringing and ringing through the quiet
        gardens,
to live more difficult passages to our line, as in the case
of death's soft clothing. What are these very dark things
growing in a pot? The most acute dots are memories
done with a pin or the point of scissors, facing the light of day
to a point on the ego. Only one barrier, of not harming,
has fallen upon the child with teeth. It's a working model
in our sleep, the imprint of a hand that was changed into a
        prophecy.
If this can only be a system, the water will close over its state,
with a creased photograph floating on it like ice.

Pastoral

By splicing information
that causes luminescence
in deep-sea fish
into grass seed,
Californian biotechnology
is catching up
with poetry.

But it is used
to enhance
domestic security:
& nobody dances
by lawn light.

After Pope

for Lisa Robertson

The bust pressure of a broken pottery ear
Must fail for a singing glitz graphology, but
Dial a breath anyway my receptor
Is silvering. In the human ledger
The liripipe is a new-found room to think
Who's atop the drive. Holding your force to my dial
Does not insist on holding your vase to my
Prior writing. When I bleed we all eat
The word pasture, have to do it—auguries
Aside—(literally) a real assignment.
Anyway I sigh manfully for actions attuning
To the renown arena. An inner renown arena musty
With seed of a wise expenditure of telepathy? I might
Goad a thinker or advocate a bottle of soda or do
What I think I forced in magic and then ate anew, lighting the
        longing
For failing. Light the shores of falling
For your row boat against stopframe forest
King Love Queen Love—what a word—till my whole
Aspen trails over bubbling waters and I'm a
Bloke and a pen originally afraid of a
Last flumy tendance. Fuck. Even my dear
Morbid quiddity's in flush camelot. Slow me now
Unspeakable oval and its consort pen
As a silly voice wails write the poem.
Please. Steal me some poetic tide, an untapped
Harvest halo to mark a human reflex,
A bullet in the heart. This very thing perceives
Each lighted stubble, stumbles, slumber
Wakes her pillows: away with the silvering in
My receptor! we are unfrocked as
Privates in the reactional republic
Of the poem's toil and in some way dissonantly
Wasting and waiting on steps still hands

Always missing a planted foreboding lungs
On the tip of the tongue, till hands always
Wrestling with flickers of gorgeous trauma
Win nothing but this button I carry
As we die

Laugh Like a Piano

after T. S. Eliot

Stunned under hotspur vehemence, odd
starlings on a garden gnome,
we waver, descend lightly yonder
glass-pure flows, your withers panting apace,
& fall then to the ground in turn
with a few gipsy mementos in your ice
bottles waving twice to some light in the air.

So a wood has hidden leaves,
so a wood has adders tanned and angry,
so a wood has letters
solely vested & boding dawn ambrosial,
as the mined desert forebodes hazard.
Ice defined
as a wave incompatible with life and death,
as a way with a boastful ampersand
& an implant faceless as a mile shaking the sand.

Sheets torn away bitter as the external weather
impaled my margin, harsh Eumenides.
Money, descend O Money! How is
a hero ever harmed in sandals, arms feeling so loose
as I wander home that they shoot a bond trader.
My shirt has lost a chest, your hand a posy.
Some tunes these cozy stations steal amuse
The rubble. Midnight. And no-one's repossessed.

Basic White

after Geoff Ward

If in the night a voice is heard
crying out in awkward passages to
confirm characters' hidden wishes,
or the struggle with time becomes buried
in the volume of utterance like snow so as
to resemble the fan of cards in a refusal
to face indulgence and strive to exist
in that regard almost fragile and fictive—
a step away from the grave passage as a trap
for the unwary casts judgment on the first
unity of politics or might have preferred
to be adept at the slender space
lamenting (as some do) direct statements
and the most compendious abandonment.
Yet we need not believe him as the figures of fogbound
signification in basic white pains and still want
surprisingly candid echoes of a serious hope
already at work within the margins.
An exercise in light may still be
a meditation on the death of a band
posing as the textual snow of a thick story
of speech, lies, and such conceits
alongside the desire of a child for the ultimate
blood built out of words like a thirst already
at work within the weapons that outstare me.

Hardihood

Change sun by sun and fling and laugh
as any spot that now had fired the waste
from the bill twitted within my brain's
winter edge, shaped in slow regret.

I wrote two letters. Given words to mine
it cuts like my table carried off by name:
touchdown will carry you back unpaid
as a vane would disjoint witchery from me.

This can of shapes from the files is a spot
when he'll come equal into the streets,
as we did with a more crashing iron fire,
a little string and a working flare pane, maybe.

Flung my iron to the bushes, to the stair,
before a cupboard. Our hands, her personal
arch stood in homespun reason's blink
burst by numbers and without the walls.

Cornered or vast, what was this green grain
to the wild eye in a ferny ring,
broached to turn with self to thin sense
between yours and mine, the sun's lip upcast?

Even no sign under her pin, steel and stone
vanished and returned on the panel.
The names had failed where the mist felt the dust,
phantom hints gone for response to open.

The name changing the barren tree
to shades of irony, rapt in the true one
to her ruin from bee slumber. Mile by mile
I come to my voice, the grasp of other.

I was like a tract on every side
as I stood in a rose spot where even the new reasoning
looked radiant, breathed all our lives
in mothy walls, under archways of thought.

Now as early measure forbids writing
I conceive laughter and a light green breath
set in unrest and small ash trees. My page
is in my space, my light like silent zest.

I claim to feel I cannot find my lack
in bespoke ends, flush within that day
your body gazed and gazed far up my stair
boring within my bones, and moved things.

Drain the light wasted by sleeves in risk,
give space stairs in secret. Nettles in your bread
by the incipient lines do indeed say green
by this and skin my cold equanimity.

2

Pronounced or heard, hid here in the late spring
while red shapes of puppets circle
and rust, I'm apt to lift you back, loving as rain.

Scarce guns in their yellow kiss stood
under the arch called circumstance
yet at that time no rent was set to the years.

Rest breaks strange stars in the waning cold
of meaning, to be still as wings. Beyond earth's doings
a father broods, speaking at a spot, and on the sky.

Last and stay, cling and greet the sick men
in blue light and dim thought of zest.
Flash out a slit through chrome frippery.

Form lies in a pinch to be ecstatic
till the image raised the plot, blind and blended
with each dome to spell cove and abrade each groin.

In the day shapes sink as ripples out of nothing.
I can recall a man who died by an alley
hurled into the sun by the bloody darkness,

And crushed like a bent tune. Extinct romance
may be silent on its long trace and count as mine,
perplexed in these late tappings and distortions.

I said iron shall perish to a shining black regret
and leave some impulse missed on the eclipse
of immense human war crimes and wounds

To life, and maybe what I believe unlit with replies.
What is worse than unanswered broods in the night
Of laws which attack life, their sleep-worker and song.

3

Opened tissues feel
one wild frame from dawn
till we go to speak

Yet she never succeeds
those millions of daily messengers:

I say some scheme tore shape
by a word flash through my land

Written on the poor unconscious flesh
that I still traverse through the heat.

4

Fear and dwindle waste the ear
No hint to fly to sense:
Ignorant skies shut earth's wide tear
And bide unreasoning yet.

Today organic dust will wane,
Be lit and unfold as this moment
Had just begun to speak
For a red cloud by the home.

When I edged a shape by this
I broke my word and left off
Biting these cheeks and bonded
With a broken time that knew it.

Between now and a guarded tongue
My face is froth, not fate:
I need to find things I knew,
A spot by no trace of old intent.

Meet me at my tread with preoccupation,
Which grew as the call for hours;
Follow my scared dead seasons
Into a thin sound screened from the eye, swallowing things.

5

In the patient world, be an instant
It subdues. Times drop their fires
And we think we drop a blind moth,
My page in space the lamp.

Know how days are birds turned to men:
Birds used to feed us shapes that cry in frost
Till delay took the shine in a mask
And the eye of strings trembled through air.

We swim on form and stony hands
As the door to less and the scarce steps:
Content is gone to name his fancy protest
Where feet mounted the will with his cameo.

Her thoughts track the sun to the lawn end
In rooms by now happier than winter:
The vent of pain is familiar, her dry ears
Wrenched to a text we half ruined.

This could have been bewitched by feathers
If thought did not cut masks with a pencil.
See that poetic water? Banks change shape best
As I look at knowledge, not you in spring.

All alight with bitter fields, the blind
Find my messenger breath gleaming red and cold
In the twigs, prone to a hurried request
To one who wrote back these eyes.

No feet bestow me where you walk beside sight,
The door emblazoned twice in the frost:
Black is best and dust has no shapes—
Matter is delight and fear, shaped in my path.

6

for Jenny

The stolen world, glowing and benighted with vision,
Ending over my ivoried task, moves and burns;
So now I draw this spot to that field in the dark
And calm all the stone time of my words.

And now the nettle did blow. It wears my fate.
I trace feet from shapes that dance
Through the night for little cost,
And shade her eyes with no repayment, no calm.

I scanned each lost child for time at his pause,
And dwindled to be left like his name:
Memory is a crumbled tree, a spectre in a mind
That may be wrong as in song the pee-wits grieve.

Now a rose and an arid silence heat my presence
Against the green skyline. She thought that voice spoke
Of my father, between dream and content,
Full of steep surprise, its curve wasted by sunlight.

Then the form of time did not return again?
Fifty years faced the dry tap and I heard Johnny's tale
In time to the wind as light dispersed the files,
And the plans I once had approached the tract of words.

The first voice was dead. I wondered what secret door
Went out through the fields beyond me. Can my mouth
Close while words lie within me? I sang the tune
We sang walking in the summer when form is fire.

7

for Jenny, again (Happy Birthday)

After all the breath, we were altered of heart
And at last each circumstance was mine,
The yew line to her every story consigned
To new lines and conventions within her precincts.

Spells of time may account for unregarded sea,
And then more times in the street,
In that long winter breath in the memory
Before names step in to my eyes and speech.

Dancing as we lay and moved like sparks
Of living ashes in a bower of breath,
I passed my heart and changed, smiling
More eyes with nothing beyond two.

What array of speech did they cover
Outside Paradise on the windows between!
Distance was a spot under the dark show
And will repeat your name through and through.

But O you, presence that fingers a close time
At dawn in sudden lines that die like a cloud,
The kind eyes, the thought with all it cannot blank,
Reached us sleeping, body and soul resumed.

8

You need no door with me, never the manifold tints
in some fancy life after a dead past. You are the spots
in a voice just the same as our note and the pale waves.

We burst in wild junction and slowed to something fled.
Time has been unflinching as rain says what a day thinks
just after noon in the mind and its phantom turns.

As a vision touches thought and, yes, bears eyes
that slip on jade to the door, to the dwelling where fire blows
and the sea pieces this finger, I still stand under the rooks.

You gaze from news of glass and smile about it between
my dim eyes wrapt in filmy time. Shift things from the table
and persist in words for circles and presences that see me.

Having said this, a trace of word paused before a splash
of dawn parted the horizon of things menaced by need
and its coppery march, till all was warm air and suspended here.

9

Who thought about her old poet and his discredited comrade?
My social ghost thought something I owned without clinging
to the gift like rain would wake me like a web from a wall.

That stone in the hall shone by his syllables. Obliterate my song
to-morrow. I forget dreaming for phantoms want it and still
the uncaring light will sing insects in the mind, peacefully.

No one touch the dazed breath on the roof with voices till my
     whim
let him ride down the long grave, wings turning in from the
     door.
The moon rose through the crack in light, a mirror of its
     shadow.

I forgot the window, emerging into the empire left by memory,
the spot of polished oak right on my intellect as if off my finger
my blustering crowd slid in small white threads with eyes
     revolved.

A whim can fail. Step behind this spot and a page appears,
     retained
in her mind this time like blankness. The poet has to pause till
her glance pervades his cover, and they must sit and smoke.

You see you put your choice on the edge of my hand. And the air
will pass daily into my arms and not perceive me. My time's
     burning
late, you marvel, and your eyes catch the voice in things, again.

10

Why should breezes glow more than my own window?
Silken waste, elms like trees there as a break
in a space of the universe when I call you up, and maybe
the word made the past an alley feather.

Sight will be my image on the eye, visible words
only being sound breathed at each face in the line.
Against each look back I nail a certain moon
as soon as the posts come to my pencil in dreams.

On like the breath, always to recall like a bright guest,
I went into the look of choice, into my ear, rushing down
to nearer to here. Between lines and no shape I heard
all this, groping after that wire bird in its voice.

By these eyes, my page was aware, my vision a shining
tragedy in string and screens anyhow. Washed with soot,
I paid for things I warned my darling of, and the figure
of the trees rises in the white voice from the leaves.

Will you take dust as a phantom mistake by the day?
This mist in me in the night was a book I made, a twist
of the drift written on my own eyes when I put it back
as the yellow space called the cloud ended in air.

11

I looked under a figure that declined a trace of afternoon
like string, like a song above new frosts and the dread coffin
on that spot far from the brothers. Ordinary thought at last.

I used to damp the light when the photograph gnawed my eyes
but the card was lost and the deed was casual. I could shape
distance like a path of white stones cut in a glass.

O here are nerves and black night, and a phantom earth!
A figure is always to be desired where the pencil knows
that irony of utter rhyme, my strange memory of stone and
        finger.

I regard others between us as the breeze, red as your day
in February, as fog hung in the eye, fog like vision in its hat
with me in the curves of things behind my back less shadowed.

In the porch I watched smartly while the household died. Old
mothers with hands frame the same moth, as if red goes away
in thought and she was coming with wings to drop down on a
        lawn.

It's not my foot, it's the skeleton of naked wires standing in the
        dust
red and slow that placed it in the string like a sanguine livery
and detached the fallen fingers we know still travel from her
        arms.

I go from my screen, from the quick waves and the white clocks,
seeing things and missing you as well as the air from eyes
in the grass, never looking across to the phantom outside the
        image.

12

When her image shone upon the glimpse, the core in sight
of the Muses would rise into the night. The next room
breathes as if it saw a red scarf and blind string fill it
till my wonder looked up and knew they spoke to me.

This has happened. At times I follow by the sea as a screen
for bared lives, tugged by eyes in the poise of one in the
      morning.
The hard sky looked over me, a bee in the sun was the mark
over my shoulder, mine to last like a vision of two pieces.

What she did, where it means nothing behind grief, I wrote
on the nettles miles from the railway. I printed the book
with casual words in the dark clock you can hear each day,
my dear, like a mood in a mask of the words I believe.

A hazed voice under the clouds would burn in the frame,
next to some doorstep, as thought prints the same things
round your bites. Ask why we called before. It was the neck.
Between the stone and my shoulders the fall of a leaf went on.

I wanted to go home, my treasure, and stand
and think in your frame just to see this face. Perhaps we
had better wish that any tune held the figure you said was dumb
and rambling, almost forgotten in flesh like living eyes.

The eye may not see the dust. I breathe your bread, hoist
my gear from railtrack and put on a story of the author.
When night comes I borrow the robe by the door,
come to my love and listen in the dark to my name.

13

Who said gambling made sleep spectral? Who wants to drown
the sun silently without a dusk where creatures rise again?
Outside the rooks rise and fall in his ear, ferns shade the wheels
behind bare time and the dancing clay in words is spectral and
    uncertain.

To know that the glass behind the dream here is stone, and the
    dusk
is this wheel outside your gate, was as if my name closed again
in blankness and we saw things dissolving in each line I read
by the poet in you. The doors will hold them in and shape the
    waste.

I can please myself like you, but the morning will rumble my
    vision
of this house. I rush to find the most austere chapter in the dust,
the whitest room you knew, as the air shapes the pale gate again
where an unknown glance moves away in irony from the rest.

14

A threaded crowd, tortured beyond fear, walked slowly
apart from where I left my windows open. A form kept on
as if the house heard me try to meet a man in the avenue.
She is a star to follow in the street by my curtains, I sang.

My tongue tried finding my love to stand in the avenue,
and I went out to a place.

Quite Right

Roosting starlings in the pink January dusk
Cluster like thoughts on branches
Outside my door and extend inward in
Vast overlapping trees of mental function.

One or two million of these
Dispositions of being I try to evoke with
This figure: anticipation and cognition are
Just everywhere as the dimensions start to fall

Out of my control like futures. I'd forgotten
The vast and besetting systems of roots
Sustaining each branch they land on, grip

And set in place. In fact, they define it in
New complexity as it gets harder to see out,
And opacity reclaims each brief transparency.

A World of Love

I

Beginning caused her tonight
her lovely air triumphing.

She beat more to make her silent
then called, 'I expect not.'

She swung away towards eloquence
in step, ice was being made

between two pairs of eyes;
just not doll enough to be a mouthpiece.

In a voice of all people she said 'Why here,
or indeed in the world at all?'

This is my experienced chiffon
cut hastily, nothing better,

the dress of her body to face
the impervious fortification

II

To be nothing left now, air or husks
gathered into a peak of languor,

about somewhere here in the room.
Minutes of intense being instead of dancing.

There had been 'writing' only
by reading the optic sequence:

but what was Jane to make of it?
She began to undress partly and partly.

Sensuous hot night, altogether spilled out,
then the word 'obelisk' caught her eye.

Death of Dance

In the world bounds become battered down
to the state. Accidents are on the spot.

Good sense in a taxi
loses its isolated public
its level dread of the universal.

The proper word, the faultless grief,
comes from the taste of people:

You are doomed by seeing in the sky.

In the Train

The slam of a dozen
on the verge of an utterance

mysterious and personal, a piece of hair
made the room sadden him

each time was to clarify everything
but the injury was haunted like a picture

with an eye full of red dusk
I was surprised that he would define relief

Shut his penetrating eye
one moment of failure to consider dead

part of himself, I know, I know,
just for an hour or two.

North

Under conditions where people wept
I stopped the car. Sleep, in fact, like a petal

he wanted simply. His eyes
had no clocks, did not turn round,

had a good head. Somebody
caught the light of justice, pale and puffy,
aggressive and quick.

"But how did you get here?" she said
like spirits at his chambers

and saw the fumy void: possibly no one
in the car. The repose of windows

the tray, the tune like this,
like some ragged and bulky cloud
stood in her overcoat.

He just wants rapid advantage;
thank him. But I think we should be better.

Living Here Now

Down by the first curtain
in the very first line
you seemed not to be denied
fire in a different key

daylight nothing but afternoon
no sign of a newspaper
forming like rivermist
you stood hands in pockets

also there was a picture
between the chair and the sofa
you had your own house
based on your own words

we think about terror
from time to time
trying to knife the bread
of cataclysm trauma and pride

it was a renewal of difficulty
the west was jagged with flames
then it all died down
and the thin air was full of today

this illusion we name ours
this one iron note in the room
makes you immortal
in the intensifying light

Mulch Tumult

for Stephen Rodefer

Munch ado about the light and the get-it-on mensch has
    captivated
like an electric shock a few people or their words which he keeps
in a jar on a shelf. Captivated, titivated, captured or capsized. If
    the cap
fits William, lazing on a sunny afternoon, chatting idly in Malay
then wear it, dear Liza, and be called to the bar of Heaven like a
    lecture
on Aristotle or more likely one on Catullus. Lucretius makes
    them go wild, too.
It's a happy birdie to use when the nightingale don't work any
    more,
and the last laugh is in yet another language. A handy way to
    drive
in old company is to take the wheel in a proper glove and just go
for a spin, dark glasses on your nose, turning that wheel of
    fortune
like a barker. Too much quotation makes you blind, my duck,
    and allusion
doesn't hit the spot either. It's the waterfall of rhetoric, the
    torrent of
inventive being in a glass house darkly, listening to the stones.
    'We should
really like to see into his head, we do it by pointing to something
    red,
every sign by itself seems dead.' Meaning something is like my
    image of him.
It might deserve the name 'investigation'. Give me your ornate
    ears, as Louis said.

Lightning Source UK Ltd.
Milton Keynes UK
06 November 2009
145920UK00001B/12/A